Modern Critical Interpretations

These and other titles in preparation

Gustave Flaubert's
Madame Bovary

Edited and with an introduction by
Harold Bloom
Sterling Professor of the Humanities
Yale University

Chelsea House Publishers ◊ *1988*

NEW YORK ◊ NEW HAVEN ◊ PHILADELPHIA

© 1988 by Chelsea House Publishers, a division of Chelsea
House Educational Communications, Inc.,
  95 Madison Avenue, New York, NY 10016
  345 Whitney Avenue, New Haven, CT 06511
  5068B West Chester Pike, Edgemont, PA 19028

Introduction © 1988 by Harold Bloom

Printed and bound in the United States of America

10 9 8 7 6 5 4 3 2 1

∞The paper used in this publication meets the minimum
requirements of the American National Standard for
Permanence of Paper for Printed Library Materials, Z39.48–
1984.

Library of Congress Cataloging-in-Publication Data
Gustave Flaubert's Madame Bovary.
  (Modern critical interpretations)
  Bibliography: p.
  Includes index.
  1. Flaubert, Gustave, 1821–1880. Madame Bovary.
I. Bloom, Harold. II. Series.
PQ2246.M3G87 1988   843'.8   87–15786
ISBN 1–55546–067–4 (alk. paper)

Contents

Editor's Note

This book brings together a representative selection of the best modern critical interpretations (available in English) of Gustave Flaubert's novel *Madame Bovary*. The critical essays are reprinted here in the chronological order of their original publication. I am grateful to Stephen Kent for his assistance in editing this volume.

My introduction considers the novel as a prophecy of impressionism, visual, fictive, and literary-critical. Victor Brombert begins the chronological sequence of criticism with a strong thematic reading of Emma's rich "confusion" of her lust, longing for money, and sentimental aspirations in an oppressive sense of suffering.

In Leo Bersani's analysis, we are given the subtle dialectic of Flaubert's art: "He is constantly demonstrating the extent to which literature renounces the immediacy of sensations in order to express them." Emma's sublime stupidity is seen in its linguistic aspect by Tony Tanner: "The fog in Emma Bovary's head is ultimately language—language in a critical state of malaise that indeed turns out to be fatal."

Naomi Schor employs current critical categories to demonstrate that Emma's true male contrast in the novel is the ineffable Homais. The philosopher-novelist Sartre's biographical reading of *Madame Bovary* is described by Hazel Barnes as being profoundly ambivalent towards Flaubert's salvation of his soul through the writing of imaginative literature.

Dominick LaCapra deftly uses the public court trial to which Flaubert was subjected so as to ask, "How does the trial 'read' the novel?" In this book's final essay, Michal Peled Ginsburg gives an exegesis of narrative strategies in *Madame Bovary,* and concludes that Flaubert's ironic stance towards Emma, and his identification with her, are equally undermined by one another.

Introduction

At six o'clock this evening, as I was writing the word "hysterics," I was so swept away, was bellowing so loudly and feeling so deeply what my little Bovary was going through, that I was afraid of having hysterics myself. I got up from my table and opened the window to calm myself. My head was spinning. Now I have great pains in my knees, in my back, and in my head. I feel like a man who has ———ed too much (forgive me for the expression)—a kind of rapturous lassitude.

> (Flaubert to Louise Colet,
> letter of 23 December 1853)

I will not echo the Lycanthrope [Petrus Borel], remembered for a subversiveness which no longer prevails, when he said: "Confronted with all that is vulgar and inept in the present time, can we not take refuge in cigarettes and adultery?" But I assert that our world, even when it is weighed on precision scales, turns out to be exceedingly harsh considering it was engendered by Christ; it could hardly be entitled to throw the first stone at adultery. A few cuckolds more or less are not likely to increase the rotating speed of the spheres and to hasten by a second the final destruction of the universe.

> (Baudelaire on *Madame Bovary*)

The societal scandal of *Madame Bovary* is as remote now as the asceticism of the spirit practised by Flaubert and Baudelaire, who seem almost self-indulgent in the era of Samuel Beckett. Rereading *Madame Bovary* side-by-side with say *Malone Dies* is a sadly instructive experience. Emma seems as boisterous as Hogarth or Rabelais in the company of Malone and Macmann. And yet she is their grandmother, even as the personages of Proust,

1

Joyce, and Kafka are among her children. With her the novel enters the realm of inactivity, where the protagonists are bored, but the reader is not. Poor Emma, destroyed by usury rather than love, is so vital that her stupidities do not matter. A much more than average sensual woman, her capacity for life and love is what moves us to admire her, and even to love her, since like Flaubert himself we find ourselves in her.

Why is Emma so unlucky? If it can go wrong, it will go wrong for her. Freud, like some of the ancients, believed there were no accidents. Ethos is the daimon, your character is your fate, and everything that happens to you starts by being you. Rereading, we suffer the anguish of beholding the phases that lead to Emma's self-destruction. That anguish multiplies despite Flaubert's celebrated detachment, partly because of his uncanny skill at suggesting how many different consciousnesses invade and impinge upon any single consciousness, even one as commonplace as Emma's. Emma's *I* is an other, and so much the worse for the sensual apprehensiveness that finds it has become Emma.

"Hysterics suffer mainly from reminscences" is a famous and eloquent formula that Freud outgrew. Like Flaubert before him, he came to see that the Emmas—meaning nearly all among us—were suffering from repressed drives. Still later, in his final phase, Freud arrived at a vision that achieves an ultimate clarity in the last section of *Inhibitions, Symptoms, and Anxiety,* which reads to me as a crucial commentary on Emma Bovary. It is not repressed desire that ensues in anxiety, but a primal anxiety that issues in repression. As for the variety of neurosis involved, Freud speculated that hysteria results from fear of the loss of love. Emma kills herself in a hysteria brought on by a fairly trivial financial mess, but underlying the hysteria is the terrible fear that there will be no more lovers for her.

The most troubling critique of *Madame Bovary* that I know is by Henry James, who worried whether we could sustain our interest in a consciousness as narrow as Emma's:

> The book is a picture of the middling as much as they like, but does Emma attain even to *that*? Hers is a narrow middling even for a little imaginative person whose "social" significance is small. It is greater on the whole than her capacity of consciousness, taking this all round; and so in a word, we feel her less illustrational than she might have been not only if the world had offered her more points of contact, but if she had had more of these to give it.

That *sounds* right enough, yet rereading the novel does not make us desire a larger or brighter Emma. Until she yields to total hysteria, she incarnates the universal wish for sensual life, for a more sensual life. Keats would have liked her, and so do we, though she is not exactly an Isabel Archer or Millie Theale. A remarkable Emma might have developed the hardness and resourcefulness that would have made her a French Becky Sharp, and fitted her for survival even in mid-nineteenth century Paris. But James sublimely chose to miss the point, which Albert Thibaudet got permanently right:

> She is more ardent than passionate. She loves life, pleasure, love itself much more than she loves a man; she is made to have lovers rather than a lover. It is true that she loves Rodolphe with all the fervor of her body, and with him she experiences the moment of her complete, perfect and brief fulfillment; her illness, however, after Rodolphe's desertion, is sufficient to cure her of this love. She does not die from love, but from weakness and a total inability to look ahead, a naivete which makes her an easy prey to deceit in love as well as in business. She lives in the present and is unable to resist the slightest impulse.

I like best Thibaudet's comparison between Flaubert's attitude towards Emma and Milton's towards his Eve: "Whenever Emma is seen in purely sensuous terms, he speaks of her with a delicate, almost religious feeling, the way Milton speaks of Eve." One feels that Milton desires Eve; Flaubert indeed is so at one with Emma that his love for her is necessarily narcissistic. Cervantes, not Milton, was in some sense Flaubert's truest precursor, and Emma (as many critics have remarked) has elements of a female Quixote in her. Like the Don, she is murdered by reality. Milton's Eve, tough despite her yielding beauty, transcends both the order of reality and the order of play. Emma, lacking a Sancho, finds her enchanted Dulcinea in the paltry Rodolphe. Flaubert punished himself harshly, in and through Emma, by grimly mixing in a poisonous order of provincial social reality, and an equally poisonous order of hallucinated play, Emma's fantasies of an ideal passion. The mixing in is cruel, formidable, and of unmatched aesthetic dignity. Emma has no Sublime, but the inverted Romantic vision of Flaubert persuades us that the strongest writing can represent ennui with a life-enhancing power.

Sartre, very early in his endless meditations upon Flaubert, sensibly observed that: "Flaubert despised realism and said so over and over throughout his life; he loved only the absolute purity of art." *Madame Bovary* has little to do with realism, and something to do with a prophecy of impressionism, but in a most refracted fashion. All of poor Emma's moments are at once drab and privileged; one remembers Browning's Andrea del Sarto intoning: "A common grayness silvers everything." The critical impressionism of Walter Pater is implicit in *Madame Bovary;* imagery of hallucinatory intensity is always a step away from suddenly bursting forth as secularized epiphanies. The Impressionist painters and Proust lurk in the ironies of Flaubert's style, but the uncanny moral energy remains unique:

> The priest rose to take the crucifix; then she stretched forward her neck like one suffering from thirst, and glueing her lips to the body of the Man-God, she pressed upon it with all her expiring strength the fullest kiss of love that she had ever given. Then he recited the *Misereatur* and the *Indulgentiam,* dipped his right thumb in the oil, and began to give extreme unction. First, upon the eyes, that had so coveted all wordly goods; then upon the nostrils, that had been so greedy of the warm breeze and the scents of love; then upon the mouth, that had spoken lies, moaned in pride and cried out in lust; then upon the hands that had taken delight in the texture of sensuality; and finally upon the soles of the feet, so swift when she had hastened to satisfy her desires, and that would now walk no more.

This is Flaubert's elegy for Emma, and ultimately transcends its apparent ironies, if only because we hear in it the novelist's deeper elegy for himself. He refuses to mourn for himself, as befits the high priest of a purer art than the novel knew before him, yet his lament for Emma's sensual splendor is an authentic song of loss, a loss in which he participates.

The Tragedy of Dreams

Victor Brombert

> *Ah! que notre verre est petit, mon*
> *Dieu! que notre soif est grande!*
> *Par les champs et par les grèves*

THE MYTH OF THE "PENSUM"

Several myths continue to distort our perspective on *Madame Bovary*. Flaubert set so much store by technical perfection, he so vociferously denied the intrinsic merits of a "subject" and proclaimed instead the supreme importance of style, he complained so bitterly of the tortures of composition and of the desperate baseness of his Norman setting, that it is only too easy to believe that the novel was for him primarily an exercise in self-discipline, perhaps even a much needed therapy to rid himself of his disheveled romanticism. The subject had supposedly been suggested to Flaubert ("Why don't you write the story of Delaunay?") to help him achieve literary sanity, after Louis Bouilhet and Maxime Du Camp, summoned for a solemn consultation, advised him to throw the manuscript of *La Tentation de saint Antoine* into the fire.

Many comments in Flaubert's *Correspondance* seem to substantiate these views. His ideal, as he confided it to Louise Colet, was to write a "livre sur rien," a book "about nothing at all," with almost no subject—a book, in short, which would exist by virtue of the "inner strength of its style." In thus posing as an axiom the nonexistence of intrinsically "beautiful" or "ugly" subjects, and in affirming his conviction that style, all by itself, is "an absolute way of seeing things," Flaubert heralded significant

From *The Novels of Flaubert: A Study of Themes and Techniques.* © 1966 by Princeton University Press.

modern notions, and seemed to point the way to some of the truly original achievements of later fiction. His own technical prowess, his supreme dedication to his art, his exigent standards all explain why he has assumed an almost exemplary stature. *Madame Bovary* came indeed to be considered a paragon of the genre. Writers admired it as one admires a lesson. For Henry James, Flaubert was the "novelist's novelist." For Zola, *Madame Bovary* represented the *roman type*.

To be considered a "novelist's novelist" is of course an enviable reputation. But the very expression seems to imply a somewhat theoretical, overly deliberate and even "cold" or lifeless creation. Henry James was filled with professional admiration for Flaubert, but he also found *Madame Bovary* morally shallow. This indeed seems to have been the slowly acquired fame of the novel: it was considered an astonishing feat of literary organization, displaying an unusual mastery of structure and texture, but a work that did not spring from the author's heart, whose subject even ran counter to the author's temperament—in short, a self-imposed task! And here again, numerous remarks in Flaubert's letters seemed to confirm these feelings. "One must write more coldly," he explains to Louise Colet, who was herself rather given to effusive writing. "Let us beware of this kind of over-excitement which is called inspiration." His cult of impassibility led him to paradoxes: "The less one feels a thing, the better one is able to express it." And still while writing *Madame Bovary:* "I am truly tired of this work; it is a real *pensum* for me now." This feeling of self-inflicted, yet stubbornly continued punishment is one of the strongest impressions left by Flaubert's letters. Thus it can be said that the *Correspondance,* admirable though it is, ultimately rendered the author a disservice. Not taking into account that most of these letters which evoke the drudgery of his work were written late at night, when Flaubert was exhausted by the unending battle with words, readers have all too easily adopted the stereotyped view of a stubborn and masochistic novelist engaged in an impressive but sterile literary exercise.

The truth is somewhat different. Not only are there sources other than the Delamare story (the *Mémoires de Madame Ludovica,* for instance, which tell of the adulteries and financial difficulties of Mme Pradier, whom Flaubert frequented long before the unfavorable verdict against *La Tentation de saint Antoine*), but the theme of *Madame Bovary,* and in particular the central motif of adultery, had been a major obsession of Flaubert ever since his adolescence. *Passion et vertu,* written at the age of sixteen years, is indeed a striking miniature version of *Madame Bovary.* Based on an actual case history reported in the *Gazette des Tribunaux,* this short "conte philosophique" tells of the adulterous Mazza and of her seducer Ernest, who is clearly a first version of Emma Bovary's lover Rodolphe. Mazza surrenders to her passion with such a total frenzy that Ernest, almost afraid (in this he announces Léon) decides to abandon her. Desperate, Mazza kills her husband and her children, and finally takes her own life by poison. The story was written in 1837, some fifteen years before Flaubert set to work on *Madame Bovary*. The subject can therefore hardly be called new or alien to the author's more permanent preoccupations.

But it is not so much the subject as it is the themes and the psychological drama which sharply prefigure the later novel. In *Passion et vertu,* literature also serves as a purveyor of illusions. The lover also plans his seduction cold-bloodedly, and almost cruelly. As for the adulterous Mazza, her "immense desires" obviously transcend the mere gratification of the senses. A metaphysical malaise is at the root of her yearning for excess. The flesh and its pleasures turn out to be an immense disappointment. The ennui she experiences stems from a hunger which can never be satisfied. Flaubert in fact compares Mazza to those "starved people who are unable to nourish themselves." Her longing for the inaccessible ultimately leads to dehumanization ("Elle n'avait plus rien d'une femme"), to madness and to an inescapable attraction to the ultimate absolute, death.

The significance of a text such as this can scarcely be stressed too much. Not only were some of the key themes of *Madame Bovary* (sterile but frenetic eroticism, sensuous longing for the absolute, flirtation with death) already fully sketched out in Flaubert's mind in 1837, but this long gestation should encourage critics to subordinate considerations of sheer technical accomplishments to the deeper meanings of the work. *Madame Bovary* is hardly an artificial or arbitrary exercise—even though Flaubert himself claimed that the subject was unpalatable to him. It corresponds in fact to some of the basic patterns of his imagination.

FIRST IMPRESSIONS

The opening chapter describes Charles Bovary's first day at school. The young boy is so clumsy, his attire so ludicrous, that he almost automatically provokes the cruel hilarity of the other students. The author stresses the boy's pathetic inelegance, his timidity, his ineffectual good will, his trancelike docility and resignation. All the physical details of the scene serve to bring out Charles's ineptness as he enters into the somnolent classroom atmosphere. He at first remains in the corner behind the door, almost invisible: the first impression is one of unredeemed insignificance and self-effacement. His hair cut short on his forehead suggests obtuse-ness. His jacket, which seems too tight around the armholes, suggests con-striction and limitations. His stout, unshined hob-nailed shoes express the boy's dullness and awkwardness. His stiff countenance—he does not dare to cross his legs or lean on his elbows, and he listens "attentive as if at a sermon"—conveys an almost servile submissiveness to authority. But it is above all the boy's headgear, a pitiful, unsightly combination of shako, bearskin, billycock hat and cotton nightcap, which sums up, in its tiers and superstructure, the layers and monumentality of the wearer's unintelli-gence. The scene ends when Charles, as a punishment for having inno-cently provoked mirth and class disorder, is told to conjugate twenty times *"ridiculus sum."*

Readers have often wondered why Flaubert began his novel as though Charles Bovary were the central character. The opening scene seems to have no bearing on Emma's tragedy, and Emma herself, of course, does not yet exist on Charles's horizon. Moreover, the very point of view of this first scene remains puzzling. The collective personal pronoun *nous* ("We were in class when . . .") evidently communicates the proper tone of childhood reminiscences. But this point of view is not sustained, and very soon an anonymous author's perspective replaces this more personal voice. It seems hardly conceivable that so careful a craftsman as Flaubert should not have noticed the discrepancy, and that the curiously oblique approach should be the result of inadvertence.

The mere fact that the novel does not end with Emma's death, and that once again, in the final pages, Charles comes to stand out in the fore-ground, should be sufficient indication that he is not a peripheral character. He is not only the permanent victim of a fate he cannot control any more than he can control the cruel laughter which greets his first appearance at school, he also serves to bring out the basic themes of blindness and in-communicability. For Charles "sees" Emma (the structure of the novel en-sures that our first glimpse of Emma passes through Charles's consciousness), but he is constitutionally unable to *understand* her. Flaubert denies himself the facile prerogatives of the omniscient author. We are gradually led to the unique perspective of Emma. But this is achieved pro-gressively: Charles serves as a transition. The mysterious "nous" can thus be considered part of those subtle modulations whereby Flaubert guides our vision to the very center of tragedy, while exploiting all the possibili-ties of an ironic distance.

It would be a mistake, however, to reduce Charles to a purely func-tional role. A careful reading of the text, as well as of the available scenarios, reveals an intrinsic interest in the character. His early courtship of Emma, at the Bertaux farm, is treated with obvious warmth. His nascent sensations of love—associated with the sights and smells of country life—are almost touchingly presented. The various drafts, moreover, insist on human traits which are far from ludicrous. Young Charles is a "gentle nature, sensitive as a young man should be." His love for his wife is deep and tragic, and it bestows upon him an undeniable stature: "ADORES his wife, and of the three men who sleep with her, he is certainly the one who loves her most [—This is what has to be stressed]." Remarks such as these clearly indicate that the very conception of the character justified his central position in the opening chapter.

More important, however, than either the technical function (transitional perspective) or the human interest of Charles Bovary, is the thematic value of his initial appearance in the schoolroom. The systematic use of character in the service of themes is indeed one of the salient traits of Flaubert's work. And not only characters, but objects also assume a primary thematic importance. Charles's cap is thus not merely an absurd personal appendage, but its heteroclite aspect, its senseless accumulation and confusion of styles, symbolize an abdication of the human spirit in the face of pure phenomena. The cap, in its very multiplication of shapes, represents the essence of meaninglessness and incongruity. Such an extension of meaning to objects is clearly one of Flaubert's conscious methods. In the description of the cap which appears in one of the earliest drafts, Flaubert states that it was a "synthesis" of all the ugly and uncomfortable headgears in existence, that it was one of those pitiful things "in which matter itself seems sad." And the cap is far from an isolated example. The *pièce montée* served as a dessert at the wedding (with its porticoes, colonnades, nutshell boat, lakes of jam, and its cupid balancing itself in a chocolate swing) or the improvised therapeutic apparatus for curing club feet (with its eight pounds of iron, wood, leather, nuts and screws) fulfill similar functions.

The opening scene of the novel is thus not so much an introduction into a given character's private world, as an indirect statement of motifs and themes. The pathos of incommunicability (the teacher at first cannot even understand Charles's name), the constriction of a narrow world here symbolized by school routines, the loneliness of the individual in the face of a harassing group, and above all, the themes of inadequacy and failure, are all set forth in these first pages. The entire beginning is under the triple sign of inadequacy, drowsiness and a passively accepted necessity. The work which ends with Charles's lamentable thought, "It is the fault of fatality!" appropriately begins on a note of resignation.

Rhythm and Symbolic Details

Two Flaubertian characteristics stand out immediately: the importance of significant details and a blocklike composition involving a double rhythm. The first chapter typically provides a *scene* (the arrival of Charles in school), and then immerges the reader into a continuum of time: Charles's youth, his adolescence, his education, his career, his first marriage. This double perspective, dramatic and narrative, constitutes the basic Flaubertian unit, and these units, in turn, provide the permanent tension between temporal immediacy and the denseness and elasticity of time. Flaubert may not have thought in terms of chapter units (the chapter divisions appear only in the final manuscript sent to the printer), but he did plan his novel around a series of key scenes and episodes: the agricultural show; the first seduction scene or *baisade,* as he crudely puts it in his outlines; the visit to the priest. The staggering number of outlines, the infinite patience with which Flaubert copied and elaborated them, is clear testimony to the importance of careful plotting in *Madame Bovary.* "*All depends on the outline,*" he asserts to Louise Colet. And, even more significantly, he has this advice to give to his friend Ernest Feydeau: "Books are not made like babies, but like pyramids, with a premeditated plan, by placing huge blocks one above the other."

Thus each chapter centers on one major subject and could easily be given a relevant title: chapter 1: the childhood and studious youth of Charles; chapter 2: the meeting with Emma; chapter 3: the marriage proposal; chapter 4: the wedding; chapter 5: the Bovary house in Tostes; chapter 6: the education of Emma; chapter 7: the routine of married life; chapter 8: the Vaubyessard ball; chapter 9: Emma's nervous illness. And the same double rhythm of narration and description is maintained throughout. Almost every chapter contains a central scene or tableau: the visit to the sick farmer, the first impression of Emma, the wedding feast, the famous ball scene, the description of the daily meals. The unique act is thus juxtaposed with the daily routine, until the two seem to merge in a pattern of repetition and uniformity. Percy Lubbock's distinction between "scenic" and "panoramic" elements in *Madame Bovary* conveniently points to the author's binocular vision; but it is a simplification, for it fails to take into account the more profound rhythmic patterns which are concerned not only with spatial, but with temporal perspectives. Georges Poulet's phenomenological approach, stressing alternating movements of contraction and expansion, brings us closer to the fundamental movements of the novel.

As for Flaubert's love of descriptive detail, it is probably the one element in his work that has met with the most misunderstanding. Barbey d'Aurevilly summed up many contemporary reactions when he termed Flaubert an "enragé descripteur." The brothers Goncourt similarly were disturbed by the importance of "props" which, they felt, choked his characters and were largely responsible for the soulless quality of the novel. Such reactions cannot be attributed merely to professional jealousy or critical nearsightedness. Many readers continue to be disturbed by Flaubert's apparently gratuitous fascination with material realities; and particularly with the life of objects.

The functional nature of the Flaubertian "detail" is perhaps best illustrated, early in the novel, in the pages which provide our first glimpses of Emma. During Charles's first visit she pricks her fingers while sewing, and repeatedly puts them to her mouth to suck them. In another characteristic pose, she stands motionless, with her forehead against the window, looking into the garden. The two basic traits of her character are clearly brought out: sensuousness and the propensity to dream. (The act of sucking a bleeding finger obviously had strong erotic associations for Flaubert: in his scenarios, he has Emma suck Léon's slightly wounded finger, and this gesture supposedly characterizes her increasing sexual frenzy.) Thus a number of details, during Charles's first encounters with her, betray Emma's temperament: her full, fleshy lips that she has a habit of biting when silent (the French verb *mordillonner* is far more suggestive); the soft down on the back of her neck which the wind seems to caress; the small beads of perspiration on her bare shoulders; her particular way of throwing her head back in order to drink the almost empty glass of curaçao, her lips pouting, her neck straining, while with the tip of her tongue she attempts to lick in feline fashion the few remaining drops.

Even her languorous manner of speaking, the modulations of her voice which seem to lead to a murmur, her half-closed eyelids as her thoughts appear to wander—all these suggest a strong erotic potential which finds its first symbolic awakening during the dance ritual at the Vaubyessard ball. The waltz (considered immoral by the Imperial prosecutor) sweeps Emma into a whirlwind of sensations, as she surrenders to the promiscuity of the dance. Here too, the details are all chosen with care: the dance begins slowly, but soon the tempo increases; Emma's dress catches against the trousers of her partner as their feet "commingled"; a torpor seizes her, and the movement becomes increasingly accelerated, until Emma, panting, almost faints, and has to lean back against the wall "covering her eyes with her hand." The obvious sexual symbolism is proof not only of the purposefulness with which Flaubert selects his detail, but reveals the extremely powerful sexual undertones of the novel which—if one is to judge by the outlines and scenarios—Flaubert prudently toned down in his final draft. For in his scenarios,· he stresses almost obsessively, and with considerable crudeness of thought and of language, the increasingly morbid sensuality of Emma. This sensuality extends beyond her character, it invades the entire world of *Madame Bovary*. According to Flaubert's sketches, Charles—after Emma's death—was to suffer from an "unhealthy love," whipped on by retrospective sexual jealousy: "amour malsain—excité par celui des autres—d'actrice—envie de la baiser."

The significant, carefully plotted detail is, however, not limited to character analysis. Indeed, this is one of its lesser functions. From the very outset, it serves as a "relative" symbol. The flat fields around the Bertaux farm, stretching their great surfaces until they fade into the gloom of the sky, represent the very monotony of experience to which Emma seems condemned. The horse's movement of fright as Charles reaches the farm almost assumes the value of a warning. One may prefer to call these "relative" symbols, because symbolism as practiced by Flaubert is rarely absolute in kind (pointing to a system of universal correspondences), but almost always of a strictly literary nature, fulfilling a dramatic or thematic role. Its function can be premonitory or proleptic as when Emma, watching the dark clouds from her window, sees them gather and roll ominously in the direction of Rouen. Similarly, when Charles carries his former wife's bridal bouquet up to the attic, Emma wonders what would happen to her own after she died. (Later she herself destroys her bouquet.) An entire moral climate can be evoked by means of such details. The street organ brings to Emma airs played "elsewhere" (in elegant theaters and salons), but transposed to the constricted atmosphere of Tostes. The unglamorous contrast is further stressed by the coarseness of the man who turns the handle, by his well-aimed long squirts of brown saliva.

The exploitation of details for ironic contrasts seems almost a perverse pleasure with Flaubert; he sometimes carries it to cruel extremes. Thus Homais, when a proper tomb for Emma is discussed, suggests a temple of Vesta or a "mass of ruins." Charles finally opts in favor of a mausoleum which on the two main sides is to have "a spirit bearing an extinguished torch." It is easy to see, however, how close the use of such contrasts comes to a moral commentary. When Flaubert refers to the mud on Emma's boots as the "crotte des rendez-vous" (the "mud of the rendez-vous"); when he has the beadle, in the cathedral, point out to the lovers a piece of statuary which is supposedly "a perfect representation of nothing-ness" and exhort them to look at the "Last Judgment" and the "con-demned" in Hell-flames—one can hardly speak of the author's lack of intervention, of his impassibility! At times, the symbolic detail serves as an ironic punctuation, as it almost graphically plots the stages of a moral evolution. The plaster statue of a priest which adorns the Bovary garden in Tostes soon loses its right foot; later, white scabs appear on its face where the plaster has scaled off; and during the moving to their new home in Yonville, the plaster priest falls from the cart and is dashed into a thou-sand fragments. The gradual destruction of the ecclesiastical figure paral-lels the gradual disintegration of their marriage. Finally, the apparently gratuitous detail can have both a prophetic and a seductive value: on her trip to the convent, young Emma eats from painted plates that tell the story of Mademoiselle de La Vallière, the famous favorite of Louis XIV. Even the seemingly insignificant fact that the explanatory legends of this glamorous destiny are chipped by the scratches of knives (how many trav-elers have stopped at the same inn and eaten from the same plates!) tends to orient the reader's mind toward a "moral" interpretation.

"One eats a great deal in Flaubert's novels," observes Jean-Pierre Richard in his brilliant essay. It would seem indeed that Flaubert had an alimentary obsession. In an amusing letter to his friend Louis Bouilhet, he himself comments on this gastronomic imagination. "It is a strange thing how the spectacle of nature, far from elevating my soul toward the Cre-ator, excites my stomach. The ocean makes me dream of oysters, and last time I crossed the Alps, a certain leg of chamois [antelope] I had eaten four years earlier at the Simplon, gave me hallucinations." Food plays an ex-traordinary role in his novels: feasts, orgies, bourgeois meals, peasant rev-els. This concern for appetite and digestion corresponds unquestionably, as Richard suggests, to the larger themes of his work: the "appetite" for the inaccessible, the voracious desire to *possess* experience, the preoccupa-tion with metamorphoses, the tragedy of indigestion, and ultimately the almost metaphysical sense of nausea as the mind becomes aware that not to know everything is to know nothing. The very essence of *bovarysme* seems involved in this frustrated gluttony.

In *Madame Bovary*, food, the ritual of meals, deglutition and rumina-tion play a particularly important role. One would almost be tempted to explicate the entire novel in terms of its gastronomic and digestive imag-ery. Sensuousness (old Rouault's taste for rare legs of lamb), a penchant for debauched sexuality (Emma licking the drops of curaçao, the drops of sauce dripping from the senile lips of the lecherous old duc de Laverdière), but above all a certain quality of vulgarity are conveyed. The Rabelaisian wedding feast—sixteen hours of eating and drinking, coarse jests and bawdy songs—is a true festival of rustic rowdiness and bad taste, the crowning symbol of which is the pretentious and utterly grotesque wedding cake. Similarly, the feast of the agricultural show, with its dirty plates and animal-like promiscuity, serves primarily to describe an atmosphere of chaos and gross inelegance.

In contrast to these plebeian *ripailles* stands the gastronomic supper at the Vaubyessard ball, with its delicately blended emanations of truffles, aromatic viands, rare flowers and fine linen. The silver dish-covers, the cut crystal, the champagne—all contributes here to the impression of urbane refinement, and sets up in Emma, through whose consciousness the entire scene is viewed, the basic tension of the novel. Her background and her lofty dreams come into such evident clash that she is almost compelled to *negate* the one or the other. Emma's choice is typical: "In the refulgence of the present moment, her entire past life, so distinct until then, faded away completely, and she almost doubted having lived it." The entire episode at the Vaubyessard ball has—we are told—made "a hole" in her life. And it is revealing that the awareness of this sudden disappearance of a given reality coincides with the degustation of a maraschino ice which voluptuously melts in her mouth.

The common onion soup which awaits her upon her return to Tostes is an ironic reminder of a reality which refuses to be thus negated. After merging with, and even symbolizing, Emma's growing dreams of luxury and passion, alimentary images point again to the vulgarity and triteness of her environment. And it is not only a specific ugliness, but the odious quality of existence itself which is brought out through images of rumination. Flaubert—witness the names of *Bovary* and *Bouvard*—is haunted by the bovine image. Repeatedly, Emma is repelled by her husband's eating habits, by the gurgling noises he makes when taking soup, or by his way of cleaning his teeth with his tongue. Just as his mastication seems to make impossible any contact between his love and her needs, so Bournisien's laborious digestion stresses his inadequacy as a priest when he fails to intuit her desperate condition.

Meals and digestive processes thus punctuate a monotonous existence which condemns Emma to an imprisonment in the self. The very rhythm of mediocrity is conveyed by cycles of alimentation, until finally the process of eating becomes a symbol of habit: "It was a habit among other habits, like a predictable dessert after the monotony of dinner." The act of setting the table is the drab ritual of life itself, with its eternal repetition and sameness. And, as if to emphasize the meaninglessness of this routine, Homais interrupts the Bovary meals regularly every evening, at 6:30, with his pompous presence and preposterous chatter.

Ultimately, the mealtimes come to symbolize Emma's utter dejection, as all the "bitterness of existence" seems served up on her plate. The smell of the boiled beef mixes with the whiffs of sickliness that arise from her soul. The image of the plate combines, in this context, the finite and the infinite: "toute l'amertume de l'existence"—but reduced to, and confined within the petty circle of her own monotonous life. All living becomes an endless erosive consumption. Food and waste (or disease) are indeed repeatedly brought into juxtaposition: the kitchen smells penetrate into the consulting room, and the coughing of the patients can be heard in the kitchen. The alimentary metaphor conveys the reality of life itself:

> Puisque la portion vécue avait été mauvaise, sans doute ce qui restait à *consommer* serait meilleur.
>
> (2.2)

> Il connaissait l'existence humaine tout du long et il s'y *attablait* sur les deux coudes avec sérénité.
>
> (2.3)

The verb *consommer* has, of course, a double meaning: beyond the alimentary image there is also the idea of waste and destruction. Ironically, Emma's very death is provoked by *swallowing* poison, and the first symptoms of her agony are those of major indigestion.

Even more ironic is the victory of Existence over Tragedy itself: life simply continues, mediocre and indifferent. Flaubert exploits alimentary images with the same bitterness that makes him grant Homais the Legion of Honor at the end of the novel. After Emma almost throws herself out the attic window following Rodolphe's desertion, she is caught again by the sickening routine of life: "She had to go down to sit at the table." She tries to eat, but the food chokes her. "Et il fallut descendre"—the very dreariness of life's continuity is conveyed by this call to join her husband at the dinner table. So also, life continues during her very agony: Homais, who cannot let slip by an occasion to entertain a celebrity, invites Doctor Larivière for lunch. (The very pedantry of Homais manifests itself earlier through his love for all manners of "recipes.") And at the end of the wake, Homais and Bournisien enjoy cheese, a large roll and a bottle of brandy in the very presence of the corpse ("puis ils mangèrent et trinquèrent, tout en ricanant un peu"). The novel ends with old Rouault's reassurance that, despite Emma's death, Charles will continue to receive his yearly turkey!

PATTERNS OF IMAGERY: HER DREAMS TOO HIGH, HER HOUSE TOO NARROW

Flaubert takes cruel satisfaction in ironic contrasts. Many of them are set up in a somewhat obvious fashion: the Bovary dog-cart and the elegant carriages of the guests at the Vaubyessard ball; Charles's smugness and Emma's frustration; her exaltations and her moments of torpor; the alternations of ardor and frigidity; Emma's vibrating body still tingling from the caresses, while her lover, a cigar between his lips, is mending a broken bridle! At times, the antithesis tends to be more subtle: the knotty articulations of a peasant hand appear on the very page where the lovers' fingers intertwine.

These planned juxtapositions do, however, point to the heart of the subject. They emphasize the basic theme of incompatibility. Their implicit tensions stress a fundamental state of *divorce* at all levels of experience. But they also fulfill a dramatic function. If Charles's father happens to be a squanderer and an almost professional seducer, if Charles himself, while still married to his first wife, is drawn to Emma because she represents a forbidden and inaccessible love, these ironies are part of an effective technique of "preparation." And these very anticipatory devices—whether prophetic in a straightforward or an ironic fashion—are in turn related to the theme of "fate" which Flaubert propounds with characteristic ambiguity. "C'est la faute de la fatalité!" is Charles's pathetic, yet moving final comment. But the notion of "fatality" is of course one of the most belabored Romantic clichés; Charles's exclamation carries its own condemnation, at the same time that it implies a debunking of the tragic ending of the novel. Rodolphe, writing his cowardly letter of rupture to Emma, hits upon the expression: "accuse only fate"—and he congratulates himself on his skillful use of a word "which is always effective"! The expression coincides with the very devaluation of love. Similarly, Charles blames the pitiful outcome of the club-foot operation on a malevolent destiny ("La fatalité s'en était mêlée"), when in reality only his hopeless incompetence is at fault. Yet who is to deny that, in addition to elements of pathos, the novel constantly suggests an all-pervasive determinism: Emma's temperament, the character of Charles, the effects of heredity, the erosive quality of small-town life, the noxious influence of books, the structure of the novel itself?

Flaubert significantly devotes an entire chapter to Emma's education in the convent. Her private symbolism of love, mysticism and death is determined by this experience. The "mystic languor" provoked by the incense, the whisperings of the priest, the very metaphors comparing Christ to a celestial lover, predispose her to confuse sensuous delights and spiritual longings. The convent is Emma's earliest claustration, and the solicitations from the outside world, whether in the form of books which are smuggled in, or through the distant sound of a belated carriage rolling down the boulevards, are powerful allurements. As for Emma's reactions to the books she reads, the image of a female Quixote comes to mind. She too transmutes reality into fiction. Here, as in Cervantes' novel, literature itself becomes one of the strongest determinants.

Yet there is, in *Madame Bovary,* a necessity stronger even than the temperamental, social and intellectual pressures to which the protagonist is subjected. It is a necessity inherent in the inner logic and progression of Flaubert's own images. The very chapter on Emma's education reveals a characteristic pattern. The primary images are those of confinement and immobility: the atmosphere of the convent is protective and soporific ("elle s'assoupit doucement"); the reading is done on the sly; the girls are assembled in the study, the chapel or the dormitory. Very soon, however, images of escape begin to dominate. These images are at first strictly visual: ladies in castles (typically also claustrated, and dreamily expecting in front of a window the cavalier with a white plume); madonnas, lagoons, gondoliers and angels with golden wings; illustrations in books depicting English ladies kissing doves through the bars of a Gothic cage (still the prison theme). Soon, however, the images become less precise, giving way to vaporous dreams ("pale landscapes of dithyrambic lands"), and to an increasingly disheveled exoticism: sultans with long pipes, Djiaours, Bayadères, Greek caps and Turkish sabres. The suggested confusion of these images rapidly degenerates into indifferentiation and ultimately even chaos, as palm trees and pine trees, Tartar minarets and Roman ruins, crouching camels and swimming swans are brought into senseless juxtaposition. Escape seems inevitably to lead to a manner of disintegration, even to images of death (perhaps even a suggested death-wish), as the swans are transformed into dying swans, singing to the accompaniment of funereal harps, and Emma, infinitely bored by it all, but unwilling to admit it to herself, continuing her dreams by habit or by vanity, finally withdraws into herself, "appeased."

The chapter on Emma's education is revealing, not merely because it proposes a parable of the entire novel, but because the progression of images corresponds to a pattern repeated throughout the book: from ennui to expectation, to escape, to confusion, back to ennui and to a yearning for nothingness. But whereas the symbolic detail is often, with Flaubert, part of a deliberate technique, this logic of imagery associations, these recurrent patterns depend on the spontaneous life of images, on their mutual attractions and irremediable conflicts, on a causality which operates at an unconscious, *poetic* level. The novel as a whole is thus constructed around recurrent clusters of images, all of which are part of definable, yet interrelated cycles. These cycles, or cyclic themes, do parallel on a massive canvas the inevitable movement, from boredom to self-destruction, which characterizes *Madame Bovary* in its overall conception as well as in its detailed execution.

First the patterns of ennui. This begins early in the novel. The eternal sameness of experience is already suggested by the weekly letters to his mother which the boy Charles writes regularly every Thursday evening with the same red ink, and which he seals with the same three wafers. Charles's working habits are moreover compared to those of a mill-horse. The primary means for suggesting an anesthetizing routine are temporal. Emma gets into the habit of taking strolls in order to avoid the "eternal" garden. The days resemble each other ("the same series of days began all over"); the future seems like an endlessly dark corridor. And repeatedly, the mournful church bell punctuates the return of the monotonous hours and days with its characterless lament. The repeated use of the imperfect tense, with its suggestions of habitual action, further stresses the temporal reality of Flaubertian boredom. Even comic effects contribute to an impression of sameness (Flaubert's sense of comedy constantly exploits repetitions): on the day of the agricultural show, the local national guardsmen and the corps of firemen are being drilled endlessly up and down the Yonville square. "Cela ne finissait pas et toujours recommençait."

The underlying sense of hopelessness and monotony is also conveyed by means of liquid images. There is a great deal of oozing, dripping and melting in Flaubert's fictional world. During Charles's early courtship of Emma, the snow is melting, the bark of the trees is oozing, one can hear drops of water falling one by one. Later, when the bitterness of her married existence seems to be served up to her nauseatingly during their daily meals, Emma is aware that the walls are "sweating." These liquid images, suggesting erosion and deterioration, are of course bound up with a sense of the emptiness of Time. A steady *écoulement,* or flow, corresponds to feelings of hopeless waste and vacuity. These liquid images of an annihilating temporality will be even more pervasive in *L'Education sentimentale*. But *Madame Bovary* also brings out this immense sadness of time's undoing. Old Rouault explains that, after his wife died, grief itself dissolved ("ça a coulé brin à brin"). The steady flow becomes the very symbol of a chronic despair. After Léon's departure, Emma is plunged again into a life of spiritual numbness: "The river still flowed on, and slowly pushed its ripples along the slippery banks." Finally, the monotony of existence is conveyed through a series of spatial images. The Norman landscape near Yonville is "flat," the meadow "stretches," the plain broadens out and extends to the very horizon—"à perte de vue." This colorless landscape is in harmony with the lazy borough sprawling along the river banks. Emma, throughout the novel, scans the horizon. But nothing appears which would relieve the deathlike evenness.

This spatial imagery clearly constitutes the bridge between the theme of ennui and the theme of escape. Once again, the series of images can be traced back to the early pages of the novel which deal exclusively with Charles. Repeatedly, he opens his window, either to stare at the muddy little river which in his mind becomes a wretched "little Venice" and to dream of a yearned-for elsewhere, or to indulge in love reveries as he leans in the direction of the Bertaux farm. The window becomes indeed in *Madame Bovary* the symbol of all expectation: it is an opening onto space through which the confined heroine can dream of escape. But it is also— for windows can be closed and exist only where space is, as it were, restricted—a symbol of frustration, enclosure and asphyxia. Flaubert himself, aware that Emma is often leaning out the window, explains that "the window in the provinces replaces the theater and the promenade." More, however, is involved than a simple taste for spectacle. Jean Rousset, in a brilliant essay, quite rightly suggests that the open window unleashes "mystical velleities." In fact, the symbolic uses of the window reveal not only a permanent dialectic of constriction and spatiality, but an implicit range of emotions embracing the major themes of the novel.

Emma's characteristic pose is at, or near, a window. This is indeed one of the first impressions Charles has of her: "il la trouva debout, le front contre la fenêtre." Windows which are "ajar" are part of her literary reveries in the convent. The image, from the very onset, suggests some manner of imprisonment as well as a longing for a liberation. After her marriage, her daily routine brings her to the window every morning. When she goes through one of her nervous crises, she locks herself up in her room, but then, "stifling," throws open the windows. Exasperated by a sense of shame and contempt for her husband, she again resorts to the typical gesture: "She went to open the window . . . and breathed in the fresh air to calm herself." The sense of oppression and immurement is further stressed after Rodolphe abandons her: the shutter of the window overlooking the garden remains permanently closed. But the imprisonment in her own boundless desire is intolerable. Emma's sexual frenzy, which reaches climactic proportions during her affair with Léon, is probably the most physical manifestation of her need to "liberate" herself. The window, as symbol, offers an image of this release. It is revealing that she first glimpses her future lover, Rodolphe, from her window. Similarly, she watches Léon cross the Yonville square. And it is characteristic also that, upon Léon's departure from Yonville, Emma's first gesture is to open her window and watch the clouds. The space-reverie at first corresponds to a sense of hope: either the surge toward emancipation, as after the Vaubyessard ball (Emma "opened the window and leant out"); or the process of convalescence (Emma, recovering from her nervous depression, is wheeled to the window in her armchair). But the space-hope is even more fundamentally a space-despair. From the garret where she reads Rodolphe's letter and almost commits suicide, all the surrounding plain is visible. The garret window offers the broadest panorama. But it is a dreary view; the endless flat expanse provides a hopeless perspective.

Chronic expectation turns to chronic futility, as Emma's élans toward the elsewhere disintegrate in the grayness of undifferentiated space. Daydreams of movement and flight only carry her back to a more intolerable confinement within her petty existence and her unfulfilled self. But expectation there is. Just as the chatelaines in her beloved Gothic romances wait for the dashing cavalier on his black horse, so Emma lives in perpetual anticipation. "At the bottom of her heart . . . she was waiting for something to happen." Flaubert insists, somewhat heavily at times, on this compulsive expectance of the conclusive event. The frustrated local barber, dreaming of a shop in the theater district of some big town, thus walks up and down "like a sentinel on duty" waiting for customers. And Emma, casting despairing glances upon her life's solitude, interrogates the empty horizon. Each morning, as she wakes up, she hopes that this day will bring a three-decker, laden with passion to the portholes. Every evening, disappointed, she again longs for the morrow.

Images of movement reinforce the theme of escapism. Emma enjoys taking lonely walks with her greyhound and watching the leaps and dashes of the graceful animal. Restlessness and taste for aimless motion point to the allurement of a mythical *elsewhere*. Once again, the theme is ironically broached early in the novel, in pages concerned with Charles. "He had an aimless hope." Images of space and motion—the two are frequently combined—serve, throughout the novel, to bring out the vagrant quality of Emma's thoughts. Departure, travel and access to privileged regions are recurring motifs. The "immense land of joys and passions" exists somewhere beyond her immediate surroundings: the more accessible things are, the more Emma's thoughts turn away from them. Happiness, by definition, can never be *here*. "Anywhere out of the World"—the title of Baudelaire's prose poem—could sum up Emma's chronic yearning for the exotic. "It seemed to her that certain places on earth must yield happiness, just as some plants are peculiar to certain places and grow poorly anywhere else." By a skillful, and certainly far from gratuitous touch, Flaubert concludes Emma's initiatory stay at the Vaubyessard residence with a visit to the hothouses, where the strangest plants, rising in pyramids under hanging vases, evoke a climate of pure sensuality. The exotic setting becomes the very symbol of a yearned-for bliss. The "coming joys" are compared to tropical shores so distant that they cannot be seen, but from where soft winds carry back an intoxicating sweetness.

Travel and estrangement come to symbolize salvation from the immurement of ennui. Emma believes that change of abode alone is almost a guarantee of happiness. "She did not believe that things could be the same in different places." The unseen country is obviously also the richest in promises of felicity. Paris remains sublimely alluring precisely because—contrary to his original intentions—Flaubert does not grant Emma access to this promised land. Her first conversation with Léon typically exploits the romantic cliché of the "limitless" expanse of the ocean, which "elevates the soul" through suggestions of the ideal and of infinity. And Léon's blue eyes seem beautiful to Emma because they appear more limpid than "those mountain-lakes where the sky is mirrored." The culmination of the travel imagery coincides with plans for Emma's elopement with Rodolphe ("il fera bon voyager") and with her visions of life in gondolas or under palm trees, to the accompaniment of guitars, in far-off countries with splendent domes and women dressed in red bodices. The very concept of emancipation is bound up with the notion of voyage. During her pregnancy Emma hopes to have a son, because a man is free: "he can travel over passions and over countries, cross obstacles, taste of the most far-away pleasures." And part of Rodolphe's prestige when she meets him is that he appears to her like a "traveler who has voyaged over strange lands." As early as her disappointing honeymoon (which, she feels, ought to have led to "those lands with sonorous names"), she knows that

Charles did not, and could not live up to her ideal of man as initiator to remote mysteries. She yearns for the inaccessible with a naïve but pungent lyricism: "She was filled with desires, with rage, with hate." Her desperate escapism, which ultimately alarms and alienates both her lovers, is of an almost sacrilegious nature. It is significant that sex is repeatedly associated with mystico-religious images (the remarkable death scene pushes the association to its logical conclusion), and that the assignation with Léon takes place in the Rouen cathedral, which Emma's distorted sensibility views as a "gigantic boudoir." Emma's tragedy is that she cannot escape her own immanence. "Everything, including herself, was unbearable to her." But just as her walks always lead back to the detested house, so Emma feels thrown back into herself, left stranded on her own shore. The lyrical thrust toward the inaccessible leads back to an anesthetizing confinement.

The cycles of ennui and spatial monotony, the images of escape (window perspectives, motion, insatiable desire for the elsewhere), are thus brought into contrapuntal tension with an underlying metaphoric structure suggesting limits, restriction, contraction and immobility. The basic tragic paradox of *Madame Bovary* is unwittingly summed up during Emma's first conversation with Léon. They discuss the pleasures of reading: "One thinks of nothing . . . the hours slip by. One *moves motionless* through countries one imagines one sees" (my italics). As for the sense of limitation, the very site of Yonville (the diminutive conglomeration in the midst of a characterless, undifferentiated landscape) suggests a circumscribed and hopelessly hedged-in existence. As soon as one enters the small market town, "the courtyards grow narrower, the houses closer together, and the fences disappear." The entire first chapter of part 2, which introduces the reader to Yonville, plays on this contrast between expanse and delimitation. The very life of Yonville suggests constriction. Viewed from a distance—for instance during Emma's promenade on horseback with Rodolphe—the small community appears even more jammed in. "Emma half closed her eyes to recognize her house, and never had this poor village where she lived seemed so small to her." The same feeling of constriction is experienced inside her house, as Emma bewails "her too exalted dreams, her narrow home." The entire tragic tension of the novel seems to be summed up in this experience of spiritual claustrophobia. The sitting-room where Emma, in her armchair, spends hours near the window, is distinguished by its particularly "low ceiling." The predominant impression is one of entrapment or encirclement. In a somewhat labored but telling simile, Flaubert compares Emma's married life to a complex strap which "buckles her in" on all sides.

This imagery of restriction and contraction is intimately related to the disintegrating experiences of sameness, interfusion and confusion of feelings, indiscrimination, abdication of will and lethal torpor. Space is lacking even in the Yonville cemetery, which is so full of graves that the old stones, completely level with the ground, form a "continuous pavement." This absence of a hiatus has its stylistic counterparts in the tight verbal and dramatic juxtapositions. There is no solution of continuity between the platitudinous official speeches, the lowing of the cattle and Rodolphe's talk of elective affinities. The seduction scene at the *comics agricoles*—a chapter of which Flaubert was particularly proud—is almost a continuous exercise in telescoping of levels of reality. Everything tends to merge and become alike. Even the villagers and the peasants present a comical and distressing uniformity. "Tous ces gens-là se ressemblaient."

Confusion, whether due to oppressive monotony, moral drowsiness or spiritual anesthesia, is one of the leitmotifs in *Madame Bovary*. Once more, the opening pages are revealing. When Charles reads the list of course offerings at the medical school, he experiences a spell of "dizziness." Riding toward the Bertaux farm, he falls into a characteristic doze wherein his most recent sensations "blend" with old memories: the warm odor of poultices "mingled" in his brain with the fresh smell of dew. *Confondre, se mêler* are among Flaubert's favorite words. "Et peu à peu, les physionomies se confondirent dans sa mémoire." As the Vaubyessard ball recedes into the past, the sharp outlines dissolve and all the figures begin to merge. Emma's ability to distinguish between levels of values dwindles as the novel progresses. "She confused in her desire the sensualities of luxury with the delights of the heart. Later, this commingling of sensations becomes increasingly habitual, until no clear notions at all can be distinguished. .

Emma's lust, her longing for money and her sentimental aspirations all become "confused" in one single, vague and oppressive sense of suffering. While listening to Rodolphe's seductive speeches, she conjures up other images: the viscount with whom she waltzed at Vaubyessard, his delicately scented hair, Léon who is now far away. The characteristic faintness ("mollesse") which comes over her induces an overlapping and a blurring of sensations which is not unlike a cinematographic fadeout. ("Puis tout se confondit.") But this psychological strabismus is not here a technique whereby the author creates suspense or modestly veils the action. It corresponds to an abdication of choice and will, and points to the very principle of disintegration. As she is about to seek solace from the priest, Emma longingly recalls her sheltered life in the convent where she was "lost" ("confondue") in the long line of white veils. The memory makes her feel faint ("molle"); and she yearns for anything which would submerge and absorb her existence. The latent yearning for annihilation or nothingness is probably the most fundamental tragic impulse of Flaubertian protagonists. Not only does Emma dream of dissolving herself in an all-absorbing whole, but approaching death is described as a "confusion de crépuscule." Ultimately, not only all desire but all pain is absorbed in an all-embracing and all-negating woe. Thus Charles's retrospective jealousy, when he discovers Emma's infidelities, bcomes "lost in the immensity of his grief." The frustration of all desire and of all hope is so great that nothing short of total sorrow and total surrender to nonbeing can bring relief.

A state of numbness or even dormancy is one of the chronic symptoms of *bovarysme*. *Mollesse, assoupissement* and *torpeur* are other favorite words of Flaubert. They refer most generally to a vague sensuous well-being, to a condition of nonresistance and even surrender. When Emma hears Rodolphe's flattering, if not original love declaration (he compares her to an angel), her pride "like one who relaxes in a bath, expanded softly" ("mollement"). The almost untranslatable *mollement* appears again, a few pages later, when Rodolphe puts his arm around Emma's waist and she tries "feebly" to disengage herself. Numbness and drowsiness occur almost regularly in a sexual context. During the nocturnal trysts in the garden, Emma, her eyes half closed, feels her emotion rise with the softness ("mollesse") of the perfume of the syringas. Her physical submissiveness to Rodolphe is termed "a beatitude that benumbed her" ("une béatitude qui l'engourdissait"). And when she meets Léon again at the opera in Rouen, she is assailed by the "torpor" of her memories.

The pathological nature of such torpid states is strongly suggested. Early in the novel, her torpor follows moments of "feverish" chatter, and corresponds to periods when Emma suffers from heart palpitations. But the real pathology is of the spirit, not of the body. Just as the somnolence of the listeners at the agricultural show reflects the dullness of the speeches and the intellectual indolence of the townspeople, so Charles's congenital yawning symbolizes his inadequacy. When the coach arrives in Yonville, Charles is still asleep. During the evening at the Homais, he regularly falls asleep after playing dominoes. Such drowsiness seems contagious. Only Emma's takes on a more symbolic aspect. She suffers from an "assoupissement de sa conscience": her very conscience is made numb. And in this numbness there is not only the principle of despair, but of death. All desire, like Baudelaire's ennui, leads to an omnivorous yawn. After Léon leaves Yonville, Emma's sensuous and sentimental frustration expresses itself through an infinite lassitude, a "numb despair." Her blinds are now kept closed (recurrence of the window motif), while she herself spends her days stretched out on her sofa, reading a book. The very atmosphere of Emma's burial will be one of monotony and sickening tedium. As Charles leads the funeral procession, he feels himself growing faint at this unending repetition of prayers and torches, surrounded by the insipid, almost nauseating smell of wax and of cassocks. A liturgical torpor invests him, and reduces all pain to a blurred feeling of weariness.

The very movement of the imagery in *Madame Bovary* thus leads from desire to frustration and failure, and ultimately to death and total undoing. Images of liquefaction and flow, which will be central to *L'Éducation sentimentale,* here also serve to convey the processs of dissolution. Emma almost perversely savors the slow disintegration of her being. The maraschino ice melting in her mouth corresponds to an entire past she wishes to negate. But the present, no matter how much one counts on it to beget change, never really disrupts the hopeless continuity of life. The tiny river near Yonville symbolizes a "time" which knows neither alteration nor respite ("La rivière coulait toujours"). This temporal symbolism is bound up with the experience of loss and erosion: the great love with Rodolphe is like "the water of a river absorbed into its bed" until Emma begins to see the mud. During her convalescence, the falling rain is the background to the sick woman's daily anticipation of the "inevitable return" of the same petty events. But it is above all morbidity of spirit or body which is suggested through fluid or soluble metaphors. From the empty and bloody orbits of the Blind Man flow "liquids" which congeal into green scales. Similarly, a "black liquid" oozes from the blisters on Hippollyte's leg. And after Emma dies, a "rush of black liquid" issues from her mouth, as though she were still vomiting. Even the soil thrown up at the side of her grave seems to be "flowing" down at the corners. This fluent quality of life points not only to mortality, but to decomposition. "Whence came this insufficiency in life, this instantaneous rotting of everything on which she leant?" Emma's question goes to the very heart of the book. For life, in the Flaubertian context, is a steady process of decay.

This relentless deterioration of everything is very different from the Balzacian wear and tear which is most often the price man pays for his tragic energy. Flaubert's heroes not only have a vocation for failure, but they fail independently of any investment of fervor. Charles's early fiasco at his examination foreshadows his entire career. Paradoxically, it could be said that unsuccess precedes the act of living. In Flaubert's world, life is not fought out and lost, but *spent.* It is only appropriate that Emma should be congenitally improvident. For she is a squanderer not only of money. In a strained but revealing simile, Flaubert compares her loss of illusions to a steady act of "spending." "Elle en avait dépensé à toutes les aventures de son âme." But it is, in reality, her own self that she is dissipating, as though urged on by the desire to fade or melt away. Flaubert elsewhere speaks of death as a "continuous swooning away" (an "évanouissement continu"). The death-wish is a permanent reality in the fictional world of Flaubert; it most often reveals itself through an almost mystical desire to vanish or be absorbed by a larger whole. On her way to Father Bournisien, Emma dreams of the "disappearance" of her entire existence. The longing for nothingness is often linked to religious or pseudo-religious images. In Emma's mind, it is most often associated with memories of the convent, with a desire to return to it, as one might to a maternal womb. The desire to stop living ("She would have liked not to be alive, or to be always asleep") corresponds to a quasi-metaphysical fatigue, to the immediate pain of having been betrayed by life itself. In the face of universal abandon, the Flaubertian heroine is driven to dissipation. She becomes the willing accomplice of all the forces of disbandment.

Flaubert and Emma Bovary: The Hazards of Literary Fusion

Leo Bersani

Romantic love has been one of our most effective myths for making sense out of our sensations. It organizes bodily intensities around a single object of desire and it provides a more or less public theater for the enactment of the body's most private life. In love, desires and sensations are both structured and socialized. The loved one invests the world with a hierarchy of desirability. At last we have a measure of value, and even the unhappiest lover can enjoy the luxury of judging (and controlling) his experience according to the distance at which it places him from the loved one's image or presence. Passion also makes us intelligible to others. Observers may be baffled as to why we love this person rather than that one, but such mysteries are perhaps more than compensated for by the exceptional visibility in which the passionate pursuit of another person places the otherwise secret "formulas" of individual desire.

Love is desire made visible, but it is also desire made somewhat abstract. We do not yearn merely for sensations in romantic desire; we seek the more complex satisfaction of another desiring presence. To desire persons rather than sensations is to indicate a certain predominance of mind over body. The sublime-sublimating nature of love is clearly enough pointed to by the notable fact that, as we see in Racine, even the most obsessive sexual passion can be adequately described with practically no

From *Towards a Poetics of Fiction,* edited by Mark Spilka. © 1977 by Indiana University Press.

references to the body. Indeed, the more obsessive the passion, the more insignificant the body may become; sexual fascination steals some of the body's vitality, and therefore partly dissipates physical energies. Love, like art, is a *cosa mentale;* like art, it systematizes, communicates and dilutes the fragmented intensities of our senses. But this is of course too one-sided. Even in passions as diagrammatic as those of Racine's protagonists, the diagram itself is initiated by a traumatic encounter with another body (*"Je le vis, je rougis, je pâlis à sa vue,"* Phèdre says of her first meeting with Hippolyte). And, even more decisively, the rich verbal designs which express the Racinian lover's passion never divert him from the single purpose of possessing another body. An abstract psychology of mental states constantly refers to an impossible and indescribable meeting of bodies. The dream of certain happy sensations sustains all speech, while the realization of that dream would be the end of speech. In its continuous allusiveness to both sensation and thought, love once again reminds us of art. They are both pursuits of sensual intensities through activities of sublimation. Love, then, can be considered as an ideal subject for literature; it is the most glamorous of dramatic metaphors for the "floating" of the literary work itself between the sensual and the abstract.

The various sorts of intelligibility which literature brings to the life of the body are Flaubert's subject in *Madame Bovary.* Character has an interesting superficiality in the novel. Flaubert's intention of giving a realistic and inclusive image of bourgeois provincial life—the book's subtitle is *Moeurs de province*—partly disguises a certain thinness and even disconnectedness in his psychological portraits. True, the portrait of Emma Bovary is eventually filled in with an abundance of psychological and social details, but, during much of the narrative, she is nothing more than bodily surfaces and intense sensations. Emma first appears in chapter 2; her personality begins to be analyzed in chapter 6. For several pages, Flaubert's heroine is a patchwork of surfaces: a "blue merino dress with three flounces," excessively white fingernails, a thick mass of black hair, the moving reflections of the sun through her open parasol on her face, a tongue licking the bottom of a glass. (This attention to physical detail can of course be partly explained in terms of narrative strategy: Flaubert economically conveys the desires of the men looking at Emma by describing those aspects of her presence which stimulate them.) Not only do we thus see Emma as a somewhat fragmented and strongly eroticized surface; when we move to *her* point of view, we have an exceptional number of passages which describe the life of her senses. Mediocre in all other respects, as Brunetière wrote, Madame Bovary becomes a superior creature thanks to a rare *"finesse des sens" (Le Roman naturaliste)*. Emma's greedily sensual awareness of the world has often been noted. The dinner and ball at la Vaubyessard, for example, provide a feast of brief but intense thrills for all her senses: "certain delicate phrases of the violin" which make her smile with pleasure, the cold champagne which makes her entire body shiver, the dazzling gleam of jewelry, the warm air of the dining room which envelops her in a "mixture of the scents of flowers and fine linen, of the fumes from the meats and the smell of the truffles."

At moments of more overpowering sensuality there even emerges a "formula" for Emma's sensual intensities, a characteristic style of sensation which, as we know from Flaubert's other works, wasn't invented for Emma alone but rather seems to be a basic formula for Flaubertian sensation in general. Sexuality in Flaubert is frequently expressed in terms of a rippling luminosity. "Here and there," Flaubert writes as part of his description of Emma's first happy sexual experience (with Rodolphe in the forest near Yonville), "all around her, in the leaves and on the ground, patches of light were trembling, as if humming-birds, while in flight, had scattered their feathers." The moon, during Emma's last meeting with Rodolphe in the garden behind her house, "cast upon the river a large spot, which broke up into an infinity of stars, and this silvery gleam seemed to writhe to the bottom of the water like a headless serpent covered with luminous scales. It also resembled some monstrous candelabra, with drops of molten diamond streaming down its sides." While the experience of pleasure itself seems to include a vision of discreet points of light (the diamond light is perceived as distinct "drops"), the anticipation or the memory of sexual pleasure frequently diffuses these luminous points into a heavier, even slightly oppressive atmosphere. In the garden description the brilliantly decorated serpent and the candelabra plunging into the water are hallucinated participations of the external world in Emma's sexual pleasure. At a certain distance from sex the thought of pleasure, or the images connected with it, makes for a less dazzling hallucination, and light now suffused with color becomes softer and thicker. After that first day in the forest with Rodolphe, Emma feels that "she was surrounded by vast bluish space, the heights of feeling were sparkling beneath her thought." Much later, as she lies alone in bed at night enjoying fantasies of running away with Rodolphe, Emma imagines a future in which "nothing specific stood out: the days, all of them magnificent, resembled one another like waves; and the vision [cela] swayed on the limitless horizon, harmonious, bluish, and bathed in sun." A world heavy with sensual promise (and no longer blindingly illuminated by sexual intensities) is, in Flaubert, frequently a world of many reflected lights blurred by a mist tinged with color. As the carriage draws her closer to her meetings with Léon in Rouen, the old Norman city seems to Emma like a "Babylon" of pleasure. She "pours" her love into its streets and squares; and "the leafless trees on the boulevards seemed like [*faisaient*] purple thickets in the midst of the houses, and the roofs, all shiny with rain, were gleaming unevenly, according to the elevation of the various districts." Purplish masses of trees against an even darker background, millions of liquid light reflections which both brighten and obscure the city's outlines: this typical Flaubertian landscape recurs frequently during Frédéric's idle walks in Paris early in *L'Education sentimentale,* and, as in the case of Emma's Rouen, it seems to be what Flaubert's "hero" finds in the world when he looks at it with sensual longing. Desire has (or rather makes) its own *atmosphere* in Flaubert.

Now as soon as we speak of a characteristic formula of sensation or desire we are of course giving a certain intelligibility to what at first seemed to be the discontinuous and fragmented life of the body. But the intelligibility is all *for us;* nothing in *Madame Bovary* indicates that Emma has the slightest awareness of a durable and defining style in her sensuality. Furthermore, in the passages quoted in the last paragraph, it's by no means clear whether the images are meant to express what Emma is actually seeing or hallucinating in the world, or whether they are *Flaubert's* descriptive and metaphorical equivalents for sensations or states of mind to which they allude but which in fact don't include them. Put in this way the question is unanswerable and irrelevant. I ask it partly because, irrelevant or not, it is bound to occur to us, and partly because it is one way of formulating a problem I'll soon be looking at more closely: that of the relation between literature and sensation. For the moment, we can simply note that even if Emma does not see the bejewelled candelabra in the river, that doesn't seem to be of any help to her in making sense of her sensations or in locating continuities in her experience. Of course, this is merely one aspect of her general mediocrity. She is inattentive even to that which makes her superior: the exceptional refinement of her senses. Emma's consciousness is intense, but it carries very little. She thinks in clichés, and, as far as her moral awareness goes, she is hardly less self-centered or more scrupulous than Homais. One has only to think how richly Jane Austen's and George Eliot's novels are nourished by all the ideas and principles of their heroes and heroines to appreciate the risk Flaubert takes in creating, to use

a Jamesian term, such an insubstantial center of consciousness as Emma
for his novel. (Indeed, James found Emma too thin a vessel to carry the
weight of the novel's meaning.) But the most interesting fact about
Emma, as I've been suggesting, may be precisely that she has so little consciousness. For in spite of the fact that she is, after all, part of a realistic
fiction in which characters have names, social positions and personalities,
she almost succeeds in existing without what the realistic novel generally
proposes as an identity. When she is not having intense sensations she does
little more than *long for* sensations. Her principal activity is that of desiring.
But what exactly is there for her to desire? In what images will she recognize a promise of happy sensations?

Love sublimates and novelizes sensation. The literature of romance on
which Madame Bovary gorges herself is the only spiritualizing principle
in her life. The dangers of this literature are so emphatically illustrated in
Flaubert's work that we may tend to overlook the service it performs for
Emma's intense but random sensuality. For a moment during the perfor-
mance of *Lucia di Lammermoor* at the Rouen opera house, Emma manages
to smile with a "disdainful pity" as she thinks of all the lies which literature tells about life; "she now knew," Flaubert adds, "how small the passions were which art exaggerated." The next day, when Léon visits Emma
at her hotel, they attempt, with the help of literary clichés, to recompose
their past, to fit the quiet, uneventful love of the days in Yonville to an
ideal of glamorously desperate passion. "Besides," Flaubert philosophi-
cally remarks, "speech is a rolling mill which always stretches out feelings." But what alternative is there to the exaggerations and the extensions
of language? In this same scene at the Rouen hotel Emma and Léon finally
stop talking: "They were no longer speaking; but they felt, as they looked
at each other, a humming in their heads, as though something audible had
escaped from their motionless eyes. They had just joined hands; and the
past, the future, reminiscences and dreams, everything was merged in the
sweetness of this ecstasy." In the same way Emma's sensual torpor as Rodolphe speaks to her of love on the day of the agricultural fair is a state in
which "everything became confused" and the present merges with images
from the past. Emma's consciousness is invaded by the odor of Rodolphe's
pomade, the memory of a similar odor of vanilla and lemon which came
from the viscount's beard as she waltzed with him at la Vaubyessard, the
light from the chandeliers at that same ball, an image of Léon, and finally
the smell of the fresh ivy coming through the open window next to which
she and Rodolphe are seated. As Jean-Pierre Richard has brilliantly shown,
a fundamental theme of Flaubert's "material" imagination is that of a fu-

sion between the self and the world, as well as among all the elements of consciousness. Contours are blurred, boundaries disappear, and the great danger in Flabuert's imaginary world is that of being drowned in a kind of formless liquid dough, in a sea of thick, undifferentiated matter. I'll be returning to the dangers of fusion; for the moment I want to emphasize that even at moments of great sensual pleasure, as in the passage just quoted, the intense sensation tends *to break down differences* in *Madame Bovary*—differences between people, between the present and the past, and between the inner and outer worlds. Thus, not only does Flaubert present Emma as a patchwork of bodily surfaces; not only does he tend to reduce her consciousness to a series of strong but disconnected sensations; he also indicates that by its very nature sensation makes a mockery of the distinctions we invent in thought.

There is, however, the rolling mill of language to rescue us. Language *de*-fuses; its conceptual nature attacks the intensity of sensations, and words unwrap the bundle of sensory impressions and extend them, as distinct and separate verbal units, along the "lines" of space and time. More specifically, in the case of Emma Bovary, stories of romance raise her sensations to the level of sentiment. They replace the isolated and anonymous body with couples sharply characterized socially, and they provide spatial and temporal elaborations—that is, a *story*—for the ecstatic instant. But, interestingly enough, Emma re-charges literary language by retaining only its inspirations for visual fantasies. Probably every reader of *Madame Bovary* has noticed that Emma "thinks" in tableaux. Indeed, the sign of desire in the novel is the appearance of a tableau. The desire for an ecstatic honeymoon is a mental picture of driving in the mountains, to the sound of goat-bells and waterfalls, toward a bay surrounded by lemon trees; the desire for an exciting existence in Paris is a group of neatly compartmentalized images of the different worlds of ambassadors, duchesses and artists in the capital; and the desire to run away with Rodolphe takes the form of an exotic travel fantasy through cities with cathedrals of white marble and finally to a picturesque fishing village. These desirable tableaux could be thought of as halfway between verbal narrative and the hallucinated scenes of intense sensations. As she indulges in them Emma enjoys a tamed version of bodily desires. There isn't a single original image in these romantic tableaux drawn from literature, but, perhaps because of that very fact, all the books which Emma has read collaborate to form a satisfyingly consistent love story, a highly intelligible cliché which imposes order on ecstasy.

Given the immensely useful function of literature in Emma's life, it is, in a sense, merely snobbish to complain about the inferior quality of the books she reads. But something does of course go wrong with the function itself. Emma is extremely demanding. She wants the intelligibility of literature *in* the ecstatic sensation. At the risk of making things overly schematic, let's say that we have followed her from disconnected sensations to the sublimating stories of art; how will she now return from art to life? There wouldn't be any problem if Emma could be satisfied with transposing literature into desirable mental tableaux. She is, however, engaged in a much more complicated enterprise, one which literature itself, to a certain extent, encourages. Literary romance gives a seductive intelligibility to the body's pleasures; but it perhaps also invites its readers to expect the body to confirm the mind's fictions. The lie of which Emma's novels are guilty is their suggestion that the stories which in fact modulate and dilute existential intensities are equivalent to them. It is as if writers themselves were tempted to ignore the abstracting nature of language and to confuse an extended novelistic fantasy with the scenes of hallucinating desire and sensation. Emma welcomes the confusion: she waits for experience to duplicate literature, unaware of the fact that literature didn't duplicate life in the first place.

This fundamental error naturally leads Emma into considerable trouble. For example, the books she reads (like all literature) make use of a conventional system of signs. Flaubert enumerates several of the gestures and the settings which signify love in the novels Emma read when she was at the convent: "[These novels] were filled with love affairs, lovers, mistresses, persecuted ladies fainting in lonely pavilions, postriders killed at every relay, horses ridden to death on every page, dark forests, palpitating hearts, vows, sobs, tears and kisses, skiffs in the moonlight, nightingales in thickets, gentlemen brave as lions, gentle as lambs, virtuous as no one really is, always well dressed, and weeping like fountains." To use favorite categories of contemporary French criticism for a moment, we could say that in this passage Flaubert gives us a list of the principal signs used in popular romantic fiction; and the referent for all these signs is love. The connection between the sign and the reality is of course arbitrary (as it is for individual words), although it is also necessary for the coherence of a specific literary system. Emma, on the other hand, sees the connection as inevitable, as a *natural* one. She consequently takes a short cut and dreams of "persecuted ladies fainting in solitary pavilions" and of "nightingales in thickets" as if they *were* romantic passion. It's as if some one expected to possess the object "chair" by pronouncing the word which designates it. Love seems impossible to Emma unless it appears with all the conventional signs which constitute a code of love in fictions of romance. Since

Charles doesn't respond to the romantic clichés she tries out on him, Emma, "incapable . . . of believing in anything that didn't manifest itself in conventional forms," decides that his love for her must be diminishing. (Rodolphe, incidentally, makes the opposite mistake [later]: unable to see "the differences of feeling under the similarities of expression," he doubts Emma's passion because she uses formulas he has heard from so many other women.) There are particular words, costumes, gestures and settings which, so to speak, manufacture passion. As Flaubert says of Emma: "It seemed to her that certain places on the earth must produce happiness, like a plant indigenous to that soil and which would be unable to thrive anywhere else."

In a sense, however, there is a subtle rightness in Emma's confusion. We can point to a tree or a chair to indicate what we mean by those words, but where is the object "love," the definite shape we might evoke each time we say the word? Like all abstract concepts, love is a phenomenon created by its own definition. It is a synthetic product (the result of a synthesis, and existing nowhere in nature), and its only reality is on the level of the sign. (And, like all conceptual codes, it is subject to historical change: twentieth-century love is not the same as love in ancient Greece.) But if love is a certain composition of signs, is Emma so wrong to feel that she won't have found love until she assembles the signs in the right combination? "In her desire," Flaubert writes critically, "she confused the sensual pleasures of luxury with the joys of the heart, elegant habits with delicacies of feeling. Didn't love, like Indian plants, need a prepared soil, a particular temperature?" But the concept of love does in fact "grow" only in the "soil" of romantic fictions. We should therefore qualify what I said a moment ago: Emma's mistake indeed *seems* to be to confuse the literary props of passion with its reality, but more profoundly she errs in thinking that passion is a reality which can be determined *at all* outside of literature. Now I don't mean that she (or anyone, for that matter) is "wrong" to use abstract words to describe concrete experiences; conceptual syntheses are as necessary outside of books as in books. The dangerous confusion is between the usefulness of a synthesizing vocabulary and a pre-existent reality which we often assume it contains. For if we make this confusion, our experience comes to have a crippling responsibility to our vocabulary, and people far more intelligent than Emma torture themselves with the vain question of whether or not certain relationships can "really" be called "love." Emma Bovary is an impressively rigorous if narrow thinker; having picked up certain words in literature, she refuses to use them a bit sloppily (which is the only way to use them) in life. "Emma tried to find out exactly what was meant in life by the words *felicity, passion* and *rapture,* which had seemed so beautiful to her in books." But nothing is meant by those words in life; they "mean" only verbally, and especially in books.

Furthermore, in seductive (and treacherous) fashion, the books which Emma reads attribute duration to the rapturous instant. Romantic love in literature may end tragically, but it is not likely to run out of emotional steam and end in boredom. Of course, all literature not only makes sense of the instant; it also makes time from the instant. The life of the body sublimated in time is the history of a person. But in Emma's favorite books history is glamorized as a succession of intensities. Romance conceptualizes sensation; furthermore, it suggests that time never dissipates sensations. Emma does experience sensations which seem to her to live up to her definitions of romantic ecstasy; but she learns that romantic ecstasy doesn't last. And we find the dramatization of this banal fact interesting only because it is made through a character who, quite remarkably, refuses to make any compromise at all with time. While Flaubert gives detailed attention to the modulations of feeling in time (I'm thinking, for example, of the chapter which summarizes the change in Emma between her return from la Vaubyessard and the move from Tostes to Yonville, and of the few pages which describe her agitated, rapidly changing feelings after she discovers that Léon loves her), his aristocratic heroine expects each moment to repeat the rapture of a previous moment. But Emma's thrilling excitements are quickly submerged in ordinary time, and it is this shattering absence of drama which wears her out, which leads her to complain bitterly about the "instantaneous rotting away of the things she leaned on" and to feel that "everything was a lie!"

Maurice Blanchot has suggestively said of Flaubert that he shows us "the horror of existence deprived of a world" (*La Part du feu*). We might consider this remark in two different ways. On the one hand, as I've suggested, Emma finds in literature a world in which to place and to identify her sensations. One could say that without literature she has existence without essence: disconnected, unidentifiable sensations on which literature will confer a romantic being or essence. On the other hand, she returns from literature with everything except the physical world in which the romantic existence might be lived. And she is finally crushed by the weight of an insubstantial imagination which has been unable to discharge itself of its fables, which has never found a world. The gap between an excessively signifying imagination and an insignificant world occasionally produces attacks of acute anxiety in Emma. Boredom is a crisis in her life because it is the lie which experience gives to the constantly interesting stories of literature. Things continue not to happen; and even the most trivial sight or sound can provoke panic simply by not corresponding to the mind's expectations, by illustrating the indifference of the world to our fictions. Jean Rousset and Gérard Genette have perceptively spoken of certain "dead moments" in Flaubert's work, of descriptive passages which seem to have no dramatic function but merely interrupt or suspend the novel's action. A Balzacian description, however superficially digressive, is never dramatically irrelevant; it either provides information necessary for our understanding of the story or metaphorically characterizes the people involved in the story. In Flaubert, on the other hand, descriptive detail often seems to be given for its own sake; suddenly the story is no longer "moving," and we have an almost detachable literary *morceau*. These apparently gratuitous descriptions have a relation to the rest of the story similar to the relation between Emma's uneventful life and her action-packed imagination. They are the formal narrative equivalents of experience which fits into no design. A certain carelessness on Flaubert's part about the dramatic significance of description educates the reader into being somewhat casual about meaningful patterns. In *Bouvard et Pécuchet*, Flaubert will finally bloat his narrative with information which we can dismiss as soon as we have received it. And even in *Madame Bovary* there are signs of his wish to train us to experience literature itself as having some of that boring insignificance which Emma is so exasperated to find in life.

Of course, one could scarcely imagine a novel more likely to exasperate Madame Bovary than *Madame Bovary*. A striking peculiarity of realistic novels, as Harry Levin has emphasized, is their hostility to literature—or, more specifically, to that continuously significant and fully designed literature of which the novels Emma reads are, after all, merely inferior examples. I'm thinking of the dramatically gratuitous and even boring descriptions in the later Flaubert, as well as Stendhal's affection for the random and unexpected detail, for a life and for books imaginatively improvised. Emma's distate for Flaubertian art can be assumed from the way she eventually turns against even non–Flaubertian art. Literature has served Emma very poorly indeed. It makes sense of experience for her, but experience doesn't confirm the sense she brings to it. And this is especially disastrous since Emma can't really return to literature. If *Madame Bovary* is a critique of the expectations imposed on life by literary romances, it is also a critique of the expectations which those same romances raise concerning literature itself. Flaubert's novel is an extraordinarily subtle dialectic between literature and sensation; the movement between the two creates a rhythm less immediately obvious but more profound than the al-ternation between exalted fantasies and flat realities.

Emma indicates her impatience with the literary imagination when, in answer to Léon's remark (the evening of her arrival in Yonville) that verses are much more "tender" than prose and are better for making one cry, she says: "But in the long run they're tiring . . . ; and now, on the contrary, I love stories in which the action doesn't let up from start to fin-ish, and which make you frightened." It's true that as disappointments ac-cumulate in Emma's life, books provide her with the "up" she no longer finds in love; unable to feel any "profound bliss" in her meetings with Léon, Emma turns to literature for a "quick fix." She stays up at night reading "lurid books full of orgiastic scenes and bloody deeds. Often she would be seized with terror, she would cry out." At these moments of terror Emma has, it might be said, finally achieved her ideal if unbearable equilibrium between mind and body. An organized activity of sublimation (literature) is providing her with extraordinary sensations. The intensities of a body left to itself are discontinuous and mystifying. Literature ex-plains those sensations, but it also dilutes them in the abstract, somewhat ghostly time of verbal narrative. The explanations of literature don't work in life, and the intensities of life are lost in the endless and tiring meanings of literature. Consequently, what else is there to do but cultivate a style of reading in which the mind would excite itself out of consciousness? To get the fantastic fables of romantic literature without the words of romantic literature would be to allow imagination to act directly on the body with-out the cumbersome mediation of language. In her nocturnal screams, Emma—however briefly and unviably—has resolved the paradox of seek-ing sensations in the airy fancies of imagination.

An unbearable and an unviable solution: in reading those wild stories, Emma is of course profiting from neither the originality of her own talent for sensations nor from the sense-making structures which literature in-vents for the life of the body. Now Flaubert seems more sensitive to the sin against literature than to the sin against life. Much of the force of a potential argument in *Madame Bovary* against literature's violation of expe-rience is lost because experience hardly seems worth the trouble. The alter-natives to literary romance in the novel are Homais's invulnerable self-sufficiency, the boredom and pettiness of provincial life, Charles's bovine mediocrity, Rodolphe's egoism and brutal sensuality, and Léon's pusilla-nimity. Indeed, even when, as in *L'Education sentimentale,* Flaubert broad-ens the social context of his fiction beyond the narrow limits of dull provincial towns, he is never even mildly tempted by the "serious" activities and institutions of adult life (such as marriage, political involvements, or even ordinary sociability). And the only characters who appear to have his unqualified approval are the inaccessible and vaguely outlined Madame Arnoux, and those mute, simple-minded, virtuous creatures, Dussardier in the *Education* and Félicité in *Un Coeur simple*.

Flaubert's radical critique of almost all versions of sentimental, intellectual and political "seriousness" could be thought of as expressing a profound distaste for all those sublimating activities which organize life in society. And Flaubert seems to encourage this view of his work by the attention which he gives, as we have seen, to the variety of sensual contacts which his characters have with the world. Emma Bovary is a sentimentalist, but her creator de-sublimates her sentimentality *for us* by presenting her both as an exciting physical presence and as having an exceptionally refined talent for sensual responses. But Flaubert's attitude toward this aspect of Emma is ambiguous. He may be seduced by the physical presence he has created, but nothing in the novel suggests that Emma's moral and intellectual emptiness and her genius for sensations have been imagined as part of an experiment in de-structuring personality. That is, Flaubert is not trying out novelistically the viability of fragmented and de-sublimated desires in the specific time of an individual life. For Flaubert, I think, finds Emma's sensations both fascinating and terrifying. The dangers of losing the self in uncontrollable fusions with the world seem to deprive the Flaubertian imagination of the leisure necessary for disengaging what I have called the personal formula of Emma's sensual intensities and allowing her to test that formula in her history. It even seems as if Flaubert were anxious to avoid the slightest possibility of making that test. The powerful deadness of Emma Bovary's environment would defeat even the most energetically inventive desires, and, when the environment is perhaps rich enough to contain spaces not yet absorbed by established modes of feeling and thought (as in the Paris of *L'Education sentimentale*), Flaubert creates a hero without Emma's energy, a figure too weak to inscribe on *any* terrain the traces of his original desires.

The natural inclination of Flabuertian desire is toward dangerous fusions; in other terms, desire leads to the nightmare of a loss of form. There are, it's true, fusions as well as a kind of material and spiritual oozing which indicate ecstasy rather than panic: the "vague and prolonged cry" which Emma hears after she and Rodolphe have made love in the forest blends harmoniously "like a piece of music with the last vibrations of her throbbing nerves," and a few moments earlier "something sweet seemed to emanate from the trees." But the hallucinated sense of substances breaking out of their forms is also a sign of terror in Flaubert. After Rodolphe refuses to give her money, and just before her suicide, Emma's very being seems to jump out from her body and explode in the air or sink into the moving soil:

> She stood there lost in stupor, no longer conscious of herself except through the beating of her arteries, which she thought she could hear escaping like a deafening music that filled the countryside. The earth under her feet was softer than the sea and the furrows seemed to her like immense dark breaking waves. All the reminiscences and ideas in her head were rushing out, in a single leap, like a thousand pieces of fireworks. She saw her father, Lheureux's office, their room in the hotel, a different landscape. She was going mad, she had a moment of fright, and managed to take hold of herself.

Emma regains her sanity only to kill herself; how will *Flaubert* protect himself from these "escapes" of being?

Only art is saved from Flaubert's pessimism about sensation and the sublimating mechanisms of social life. The Flaubertian cult of art explains Flaubert's severity toward inferior art. The realistic claims of Emma's favorite novels depend on their ignoring their own mediating processes, on their attempt to hide the differences between the nature of the intensities they seem to exalt and that of the exalting narrative itself. As I've said, they encourage Emma to search in life for the abstractions invented in books, and they also invite her to expect that real time, like the printed time of a novel, can be an uninterrupted succession of intense passages. Emma contributes to the sins of literary romance and, in a way, skilfully dimisses art by trying to separate the romance from the literature and thereby ignoring the work—the effort and the product—of the writer. She brings to these books exactly what they require: a lack of imagination. She reads literature as we might listen to a news report. Emma Bovary parodies all the pious claims which have been made by realism in Western esthetics for the relevance of art to life. Down-to-earth even in the midst of her raptures, Emma "had to be able to extract from things a kind of personal profit; and she rejected as useless everything which didn't contribute to the immediate gratification of her heart,—being by temperament more sentimental than artistic, seeking emotions and not landscapes."

Flaubert's writing is a continuous correction, through stylistic example, of Emma's confusions. The book we are reading constantly draws our attention to its own nature as a *composed* written document. Flaubert speaks in his correspondence of moments when he himself is, as it were, so taken in by the realism of his own writing that he begins to experience the incidents he describes: he shares both Emma's and Rodolphe's sensations in the scene of their love-making in the forest, and he writes the section on Emma's death with the taste of arsenic in his mouth. Occasionally Flaubert thus tends to draw from his own writing something like the immediate "personal profit" which Emma demands from literature. But to spend a couple of weeks shaping a single paragraph hardly seems calculated to leave the writer capable of "seeing through" his writing to the experiences it describes. The painfully slow composition of *Madame Bovary* is much more likely to leave Flaubert with the taste of verbal agonies rather than with the taste of arsenic.

More importantly, Flaubert's language, unlike Stendhal's, calls attention to its own strategies, sounds and designs. Flaubert's text has kept traces of being continuously worked over; and while this gives something awkward and heavy to his writing (which, in my previous work on Flaubert, I now think I've tended to over-emphasize), we might also feel that a certain stylistic opacity is Flaubert's decisive refutation of Emma's confused argument for a literature of pure sensation. The very fact that, because of Emma's sensuality, Flaubert has so often to describe moments of intense sensation gives him frequent occasions for illustrating the "proper" literary use of sensation. And what Flaubert shows us is a detailed process of establishing intervals within sensations of fusion which seem to allow for no intervals. In the passage I quoted some time ago, which describes Emma and Rodolphe's last night together, Flaubert compares the reflection of the moon in the water to a "headless serpent covered with luminous scales," and also to an enormous candelabra with drops of molten diamond flowing down its sides. The sexual suggestiveness of these images is obvious. As I've said, they transpose Emma's sensual pleasure into a hallucinated scene in the external world. But also, by the very fact of being literary images, they are the sign, for us, of a certain distance from the sensations they describe. In her sexual exaltation, Emma may actually *see* the serpent and the candelabra; a much cooler novelist tells us that the moon's light "seemed to writhe to the bottom of the water like a headless serpent covered with luminous scales," and then, somewhat awkwardly, he starts the second comparison (in a new sentence) with: "It also resembled . . ." These last few words could have been eliminated; we might have had a single sentence, with the two images closer to each other. "It also resembled [*cela ressemblait aussi à*]" is a heavy but salutary reminder of the *work* of comparison. To make a verbal analogy is to bring together two things which may usually not go together, but at the very instant we say the second term of the analogy we establish a difference between it and the first term. We create a linguistic space which no similarity can abolish.

Writing is the creation of such intervals, spaces, and differences. To speak and to write are the sublimating activities which allow us to spread out sensations in time and in space. Flaubert, whose terror of sensual fusions seems to have made this a literally saving truth, makes the point for us in more extreme ways than most other writers. Comparisons can be particularly obtrusive in his work; a somewhat creaky machinery for making analogies almost mangles the object of comparison. In a famous and frequently derided analogy Flaubert compares Emma's memory of Léon to an abandoned campfire in the snow of a Russian steppe, and by the end of the second paragraph of an extravagantly extended comparison, there is some question of whether or not Emma's anguish is going to survive this exercise in Slavic meterology. Proust, in an often quoted remark, declared that there is not a single beautiful metaphor in all Flaubert. But the presumed "real' point of departure for a Proustian comparison is, as in Flaubert, but even more frequently than in Flaubert, volatilised and absorbed into the imaginative logic of a process of composition. What is not "beautiful" in Flaubert is not the content of his metaphors but the glaring visibilty of his literary strategies. He is far more concerned than Proust, perhaps because of those terrors of the sensual imagination which we have briefly looked at, in maintaining a sharp distinction between art and the rest of life. The heaviness of much of his writing could therefore be thought of as pedagogically useful: he is constantly demonstrating the extent to which literature renounces the immediacy of sensations in order to express them.

As an example of those fusions which take place in Flaubert at moments of great sensual excitement, I've spoken of the passage which decribes Emma's sensual torpor in the city hall of Yonville on the day of the agricultural fair. Present and past, Rodolphe and Léon, the odor from the viscount's beard and the odor from Rodolphe's hair merge into a single swimming sensation. "The sweetness of this sensation [of smelling Rodlophe's pomade] thus penetrated her desires from the past, and like grains of sand in a gust of wind, they swirled in the subtle breath of the perfume which was spreading over her soul." Everything has merged into a single, indistinct, whirling sensation—everything, that is, except the only thing we are really given, which is this exceptionally complex sentence. And the coherence of the sentence depends on our moving carefully from one distinct unit to the other in order to follow the construction of Flaubert's metaphor. The sentence begins with a kind of abstract chemistry, suddenly switches to the concrete image of sand in the wind, which seems to authorize the verb "swirled [*tourbillonnaient*]" when we return, in the last part, to the penetration and dancing of past desires in a present sensation. As even these brief remarks indicate, the fusions of literature are always separations or articulations, and they invite the critic to even further articulations. The Flaubertian workshop is one in which a master craftsman—somewhat at the expense of his own craft—teaches us to read.

The "Morselization" of Emma Bovary

Tony Tanner

"Ah yes!" returned Félicité. "You're like Guérin's daughter, the fisherman at Le Pollet, that I knew at Dieppe before I came to you. She was that wretched, you'd think to see her standing in the doorway there was funeral pall hung up over the door. It seems she'd got a sort of fog in her head, the doctors couldn't do a thing with her, and no more could the *curé*. When she got it real bad she'd go off by herself long the beach, and the coast-guard often used to find her there on his rounds. Stretched flat out on the shingle she'd be, crying her eyes out. . . . They say it went when she got married, though."

"But with me," replied Emma, "it didn't come on till I was married."

(—Ah! oui, reprenait Félicité, vous êtes justement comme la Guérine, la fille au père Guérin, le pêcheur du Pollet, que j'ai connue à Dieppe, avant de venir chez vous. Elle était si triste, si triste, qu'à la voir debout sur le seuil de sa maison, elle vous faisait l'effet d'un drap d'enterrement tendu devant la porte. Son mal, à ce qu'il paraît, était une manière de brouillard qu'elle avait dans la tête, et les médecins n'y pouvaient rien, ni le curé non plus. Quand ça la prenait trop fort, elle s'en allait toute

---

From *Adultery in the Novel: Contract and Transgression.* © 1979 by The Johns Hopkins University Press, Baltimore/London.

43

seule sur le bord de la mer, si bien que le lieutenant de la dou-
ane, en faisant sa tournée, souvent la trouvait étendue à plat
ventre et pleurant sur les galets. Puis, après son mariage, ça lui
a passé, dit-on.

    —Mais, moi, reprenait Emma, c'est après le mariage que ça
m'est venu.)

(Madame Bovary)

[At] Emma's first appearance in the book, she is first perceived on the
threshold ("sur le seuil"), that liminal area of indeterminacy where the
Guérin girl languished in a melancholy of transition and uncertainty (see
the quotation [above]). She is wearing a blue dress with three flounces
("trois volants"); as I have said [elsewhere], things in general tend to fall
in threes about her. Her initial environment is the kitchen, where she is
surrounded by the usual utensils—but so described as to seem somewhat
menacing and disproportionately huge, hard, and shining ("all of colossal
size and shone like polished steel"; "tous de proportion colossale, brillaient
comme de l'acier poli"), with something potentially percussive and even
aggressive about them ("an array of kitchen utensils"; "une abondante batterie de cuisine"—but *batterie* has a harsher aura to it than *array*). There is
also a large fire, and some wet clothes drying out. Fire and water produce
steam or mist (wet clothes and sheets are referred to more than once in
the book), and the softness and moistness of the clothes contrasts with the
gleaming polished metallic surfaces of the instruments that are so obtru-
sively present. In such oppositions and minglings of textures and elements,
Emma was, effectively, incubated, and in different forms they will determine the shape of her subsequent life, which is endlessly involved in permutations of clothes, "metallicism" or threatening male "instruments" of
various kinds, and water—all existing in different relationships to the central fire of her urgent and uncertain appetites, her clamorous and indefin-
able desires.

    That is an appearance and a setting: the paragraph contains no men-
tion of any movement on Emma's part. The first time she is described as
doing something—so that the static appearance takes on the dimension of
activity—occurs when Charles is attending to her father's fracture. She is
trying to sew. "Mademoiselle Emma tried to sew some pads. She was so
long finding her work-box that her father lost patience with her. She made
no answer; but as she sewed she pricked her fingers, and then she put them
to her mouth and sucked them." ("Mlle. Emma tâchait de *coudre* des *cous-*

sinets. Comme elle fut longtemps avant de trouver son étui, son père s'impatienta; elle ne répondit rien; mais tout en cousant, elle se piquait les doigts, qu'elle portait ensuite à sa bouche pour les sucer" [my italics].) This is something more than a cameo of harmless domestic incompetence. At this point I just want to stress that the attempt to sew (construct, make up, put together, assemble, etc.) is faulty and results in a slight self-puncturing, a minute but perceptible hint of breaking into or interrupting the smooth continuity of the bodily surface. Emma is indeed a long time in finding her "work-box"—étui, a case, box, or cover—and her life is to be paradoxically both a continual encasement and a prolonged uncovering. Her father is impatient but powerless and helpless; she no longer has to speak to the father (her relationship to him may be said to have been fixed at the stage indicated by her drawing of Minerva [sic!] hung in the living room and signed [in Gothic letters] "A mon cher papa"). Instead she puts her fingers to her mouth and sucks them. There is no need to underline the suggestiveness of this self-suckling action, but even though these little aspects of her behavior may pass almost unnoticed as being entirely within the range of average and normal daily behavior in the house, I would suggest that just as the pricking of the fingers carries latent hints of self-piercing, so this sucking of the fingers adumbrates an appetitive drive that will only finally be satisfied by devouring the self (Emma's terminating act is precisely once again to put her fingers to her mouth; this time, of course, carrying poison—but the morphology of the gesture is the same). And the puncturing of Emma's skin is continued after her death by no less an agent than M. Homais, for when Charles asks for a lock of Emma's hair, it is Homais who takes the scissors, but "he was shaking so violently that he punctured the skin in several places" ("il tremblait si fort, qu'il piqua la peau des temps en plusieurs places").

So far Emma has been depicted in terms of dress and setting and this activity of attempted sewing. It is then that her physical being begins to emerge, item by item, or, as we say, bit by bit. We may infer that the syntagmatic relationship between one part of the body and the next corresponds to the movements of Charles's attention as his eyes take in one feature after another, but we must also recognize that the sequence (and thus the separation) of features is also an aspect of the text itself. This is the sequence in which Emma's physical presence is perceived/established, either prefaced by a statement concerning Charles as the perceiver, or simply asserted by the text: her nails, her hands, her finger joints or knuckles (*phalanges* is a fairly technical word and is appropriate to Charles's "medical" perspective—Emma is being anatomized), her eyes, her lips, then her neck, her hair, the curve of her skull ("courbe de crâne," again a rather cold, professional term), the tips of her ears, her temples, her cheekbones ("pommettes"), her shoulder. In the remainder of this first short scene the only other references to her person are to "le front" and "le dos" (forehead, but also more generally, the "front-ing" part, and the back). In the middle of this description/anatomization Charles is invited by Emma's father "to take a bite" ("à prendre un morceau"). The italicization of a phrase so that it is visibly discontinuous with the surrounding text is of course a polysemic device; among the different effects it can achieve, one is to mark a phrase, not just as a cliché and a common saying, but as an importation or implantation of a saying from one context to another. Thus prendre un morceau is a phrase generally applied not just to taking a bite but to taking a bit, in any one of potentially innumerable contexts. For example, it certainly indicates a similarity of attitude to food and to women. (Homais, we later learn, "in the matter of physical qualities was not averse from a slim morsel" ["quant aux qualités corporelles, ne détestait pas le morceau"]). Again the word is italicized—it is the commonest currency in that context; it is the accepted word to say. Once again the empty word proclaims itself through the empty man. The phrase thus becomes another borrowed pattern, endlessly duplicating itself in the mouths of differing speakers. Being nonspecific (just "un morceau"), it becomes a general and generalizing activity and thus a homogenizing one. The cliché maps the conduct, and thus one and the same mode of mindless appropriation may be indifferently applied in widely differing contexts. Take a bit—of whatever, or whomsoever.

I have referred [elsewhere] already to the process of "morselization" in which Emma seems to get progressively involved, so that by the end she is indeed in every way morcelée; I would now suggest that we witness an epitome of this process in this first description of her appearance. She is "morcelized" by Charles's eye and by Flaubert's text. Alike, they register the parts with careful and minute attention, but precisely in doing so they miss the whole, which is not to be found in the sum of the separate items. The difference, if I may put it this way, is that Charles does not know this, while Flaubert does. Morselization is inherent in the act of writing. Detailing is dismembering. One might want to make the obvious objection that the breaking up and reassemblage of features that can be practiced in endless permutations at the level of language, is precisely not to be confused with the irreversible corporeal fragmentations of a single body. But I think Flaubert intends us to become aware of the processes by which this apparently neutral activity of language *can* in fact impinge on the body—both as speech and writing—and intrude its dis-integrative and de-structive potentialities into the vulnerable wholeness of the human organism. It is merely a truism to observe that language disintegrates and destructures the continuum of the world, only to reintegrate and restructure it at another level in another medium. Emphasis and context are what matter, and here, it seems to me, Flaubert is revealing Emma Bovary to us as a locus of morselization, a process variously conducted by the author, the men around her, and herself. (Thus, she already reveals a habit of biting her lips in her silent moments, but I want to return to that description.) Something of what I think is present in what Flaubert is doing in this interplay between linguistic and physical atomization may be conveyed by a remarkable passage in one of Lacan's essays, in which he describes the "mystery of the signifier" ("mystère du signifiant") and imagines it making the following statement concerning its own powers. "So runs the signifier's answer, above and beyond all significations: 'You think you act when I stir you at the mercy of the bonds through which I knot your desires. Thus do they grow in force and multiply in objects, bringing you back to the fragmentation of your shattered childhood [au morsillement de ton enfance déchirée]. So be it: such will be your feast until the return of the stone guest I shall be for you since you call me forth.' " One achievement of Flaubert's book is to bring Emma back precisely "au morcellement de [son] enfance déchirée" ("Seminar on 'The Purloined Letter' ").

The morselizing process is repeated, textually, on Emma's deathbed, when we are given an account of the priest dipping his right thumb in the oil and applying extreme unction, touching the various parts of her body in sequence—first on the eyes, then on the nostrils, then on the mouth, then on the hands, and lastly on the soles of her feet. After the mention of each part Flaubert adds an amplifying comment—e.g., "lastly on the soles of the feet that once had run so swiftly to the assuaging of her desires, and now would walk no more" ("enfin sur la plante des pieds, si rapides autrefois quand elle courait à l'assouvissance de ses désirs, et qui maintenant ne marcheraient plus"). The cumulative effect of these amplifying comments, balanced one with the next, is somewhat sententious, even liturgical. But this is appropriate, for while the priest dips his thumb in the oil and touches the parts of Emma's body, intoning the appropriate prayers, Flaubert dips his pen in his ink and likewise touches on the parts of Emma's body and adds his own litany. Author, priest, husband, seducer, lover—all see her partially, in parts, and take her apart, in different ways. Flaubert's

itemizing/atomizing continues to the moment of her death, thus also enact-
ing the painful disassembly and disintegration of the body. Near the end
her tongue effecty disengages itself from her body completely—"the
whole of her tongue protruded from her mouth" ("La langue tout entière
lui sortit hors de la bouche"). Earlier her jaws were described as moving
"as though she had a heavy weight on her tongue" ("comme si elle eût
porté sur la langue quelque chose de très lourd"), and we may say that
among other things it is the heavy weight of language itself she has been
carrying. Like Charles Bovary and everyone, of course, but Emma's is the
exemplary case. She is the figure who is unstable linguistically, as she is
domestically and socially; her virtue "totters" in the cathedral as her speech
"stutters" in and after the theater, and her attempts at sewing result in
pricked fingers. She cannot properly handle what she has to work with.
As her tongue leaves her head, Emma effectively disgorges the weight of
language that she could never quite carry in a way that would make for a
balanced, unvertiginous life. The last parts of her body to be singled out
are her hair and eyes, as they were singled out at the beginning. After this
her morselization is complete, definitive.

There is one other aspect of the itemization of Emma's features and
appearance I wish to note. She is described as carrying a pair of tortoise-
shell eyeglasses attached to her bodice "comme un homme" ("in masculine fashion"). The male world is constantly looking at Emma in various
kinds of detached, calculating fashions, whether it is Charles's slow examination of her anatomical features, Rodolphe's instant undressing of her in
his mind's eye, or Flaubert's "dispassionate" detailing of her life and death.
(Justin's adoring gaze is an exception.) Spectacles are often used in literature to imply a particular kind of scrutiny (myopic, unfeeling, ruthlessly
analytic, etc.), and we may say that while Emma appears not to use her
glasses (indeed from some points of view has exceedingly poor vision and
prefers the blurred far to the oppressively clear proximate), she herself is
constantly being looked at in different ways by the male world, not only
"seen" but "seen not seeing" and even "seen seeing herself not being seen"
("vu ne pas voir" "vu se voyant n'être pas vu") (Lacan). She is not only
under the tyranny of the male word, as I tried to suggest [elsewhere]; she
is under the related tyranny of the male eye (a kind of ocular sadism); and
she wears, unwittingly, a badge of her bondage as part of her costume.

I now want to quote two other details given us in this first "look" at
the front and back of Emma Bovary. The first is while Charles is duly
"taking a bite" (though no *food* is mentioned, an unusual absence in this
book, perhaps to make us consider what exactly Charles is being invited

to take a bit/bite *of.* "The room was chilly, and she shivered as she ate, revealing then something of her full lips, which she had a habit of biting in her silent moments." "Comme la salle était fraiche, elle grelottait tout en mangeant, ce qui *découvrait* un peu ses lèvres charnues, qu'elle avait *coutume* de mordilloner à ses moments de silence. Son *cou* sortait d'un col blanc, rabattu" [my italics]). The second detail occurs when Charles is about to leave and is looking for his whip. Emma stoops to pick it up, and Charles makes a move to help and a decisive and *determining* contact is made. "He felt his chest brush against the girl's back, bending beneath him. She got up red in the face, and looked at him over her shoulder as she handed him the lash." ("Il sentit sa poitrine effleurer le dos de la jeune fille, *courbée* sous lui. Elle se redressa toute rouge et le regarda par-dessus l'épaule, en lui tendant son nerf de boeuf" [my italics].) These bodily responses have their own eloquence, and they seem to foreshadow many of Emma's subsequent actions and reactions, which may be seen as mutations on these early involuntary gestures. Thus her "nibbling" (rather than "biting") of her own lips during her silences adumbrates her ultimately self-devouring attempts to find something to consume to fill up the gaps ("boucher les interstices") in her conversation, her consciousness, her life. (And note that this was a habit indulged in by Charles's mother—thus, "Mme. Bovary se mordait les lèvres"; it is another repetition, a duplication of habit—not a genetically transmitted quality, but rather a sort of borrowed pattern of response that keeps recurring in that recursive society. As Emma grows up she will graduate from nibbling to biting, as others have before her.) The handing of the whip to the fumbling Charles is a gesture that indeed speaks for itself, and the blush that suffuses Emma's face when her back brushes against Charles's chest is the established signal for the arousal of some latent sexuality (an erection of the head is, I think, how Freud describes the blush). But it is her stance that is, if anything, even more decisive. She is "bending beneath him" ("courbée sous lui"), a position not simply suggesting the sexual dominance of the male (a dominance surely very imperfectly asserted by the meek, compliant Charles), but more generally the inevitable female submission to the matrix of the male world around her. She must and can only "bend" under it to the shapes, postures, and positions that it offers, imposes, or dictates. Thus her bodily curves offer themselves for the curvings (social and sexual) of the men who will form (and deform) her life.

I have so far drawn attention to a series of words in this scene which have a similar root morpheme, or "radical"—*coudre, coussinets, couvrir, coutume, courbée,* and *cou* (for the relationship between roots and radicals see

Saussure, *Course in General Linguistics*). Let me add to this group some further instances in the book of words containing the same root or a similar
syllable. *Coutume* recurs, as in the phrase "tout rentrait dans la coutume"
("things reverted to normal"), or in the verb *s'accoutumer*. The decisive argument used to persuade Hippolyte to undergo the operation to cure him
is "*c'est que ça ne lui coûterait rien*" ("it would not cost him anything").
There are a number of references to both *coups* ("blows," "knocks") and
coudes ("elbows")—sometimes these are literal, as when a boy knocks
Charles's cap to the floor with "un coup de coude," or they may be metaphorical, as when Emma is stunned by Lheureux's threats and sinks back
as if from a "coup de massue" ("knock-out blow"). Emma yearns and
loves to run ("elle eut envie de courir"), even if it is finally in circles; this
in turn produces not only giddiness but exhaustion, "courbature" (at times
she feels as if she would like to sleep forever). There is play on the very
close assonance of *cour* ("court," "yard") and *coeur* ("heart"), as in the following passage concerning Rodolphe: "car les plaisirs, comme des écoliers
dans la cour d'un collège, avaient tellement piétiné sur son coeur, que rien
de vert n'y poussait" ("for his pleasures had so trampled over his heart,
like schoolboys in a playground, that no green thing grew there"). Where
the almost-identity of sound perfectly signals Rodolphe's inability to distinguish a common playground from what is traditionally considered the
inmost sanctuary of private feelings. It is his *letter* ("ta lettre") that, Emma
insists, "tore my heart in two" ("elle m'a déchiré le coeur!"), another indication of the power of the word to penetrate and mutilate the body. Inevitably in a book concerning a society so obsessed with clothes there are
frequent references to "costume." Emma imagines how she would have
embroidered Lagardy's costumes ("brodant elle-même ses costumes"), and
the more desperately she commits herself to the final stages of adultery the
more recourse she has to "coquetteries du costume." It is, as I have mentioned [elsewhere], one of the paradoxes of her experience that at the same
time as she is getting more and more involved in coquetries of costume
and, as it were, pointlessly multiplying her wardrobe, she has an increasing compulsion to throw off all the costumes, as if in quest of some ultimate nakedness. Thus in a famous passage, "She snatched off her dress
and tore at the thin laces of her corsets, which whistled down over her
hips like a slithering adder . . . then made a single movement and all her
clothes fell to the floor." ("Elle se déshabillait brutalement, arrachant le la-
cet mince de son corset, qui sifflait autour de ses hanches comme une couleuvre qui glisse . . . puis elle faisait d'un seul geste tomber ensemble tous
ses vêtements.") The element of brutality that is entering into Emma's

treatment of her own clothes and body is an indication of her accelerating desperation. The simile of the snake is often remarked upon, and it of course has ramifying resonances. Among other things, it introduces a kind of serpentine life to Emma's clothes, an autonomous erotic vitality acquired or displaced from her body. In this connection consider another simile in which she encircles herself (again the ubiquitous *comme*). It is a transcription of her attitude to Charles. "Was not he the very obstacle to all felicity, the cause of all her wretchedness, the pointed buckle, as it were, on the complicated strap that bound her" ("N'était-il pas, lui, l'obstacle à toute félicité, la cause de toute misère, et comme l'ardillon pointu de cette courroie complexe qui la bouclait de tous côtés?"). We may note here again the root echo in *cou*leuvre and *cou*rroie, though this time the simile originates from Emma. That is to say, that just as her life is increasingly permeated with clothes, so clothing permeates her thinking; Charles is registered as the pointed buckle-tongue, and her situation in general as "cette courroie complexe." She is seeing her life in terms of costume. And if she registers her position as being like a "complex belt" where the circle is rigid, closed, a stifling constraint, then she may well seek to shake and wriggle herself out of it as and when she can, thereby exchanging the dead sign of bondage (*courroie*) for a living, spiraling, sign of release (*couleuvre*). Such moments of release/undress are inevitably temporary, and there is always the return to ever more "costume" and the ever-tightening *courroie complexe*.

It would be possible to point to other words with the *cou* root used in the account of Emma's appearance and behavior (*secouer* and *couper* or *découper* figure among her movements and actions for instance), but I want to return to two of them that occurred in the account of her first appearance and that recur again in the later and final stages of her life. As I said, she is first seen trying, not very successfully, to sew ("tâchait de coudre," "tout en cousant"). In the chapter following what is effectively her complete capitulation to adultery (the carriage ride in Rouen), she is described, back in her home, in an act of un-sewing. "She was unstitching the lining of a dress; bits of stuff lay scattered all around her." ("Elle décousait la doublure d'une robe, dont les bribes s'éparpillaient autour d'elle.") I have commented before [elsewhere] on the accumulating "privatives" in the account of Emma's life, and *décousait* is one of the most significant of all. Emma is unstitching the lining of the garment (covering) of her life. Adultery "unstitches" marriage; Emma is unstitching everything, including herself, and the bits are indeed scattered around her. In unstitching the costume that is her social existence, Emma is at the same time unraveling custom—and she never thinks to count the cost. In a very profound sense custom is costume, and customs are what it costs to be part of a community (hence the importance of the Customs House in Hawthorne's novel of adultery, *The Scarlet Letter*). Custom and costume, both in English and French, derive from *consuescere,* the Latin for "to accustom," just as the English *consuetudinary* and the French *coutumier* can be both adjectives meaning "customary," and nouns referring to a book or collection of customs. "Coudre" is thus a primal activity that both literally and metaphorically creates costumes/customs. By marking her imperfect mastery of this distinctly and distinguishingly human activity from the start, Flaubert can make us aware of a continuity and relatedness between all Emma's uncertainties, instabilities, and incompetencies—in marriage, in money, in language, in love. She cannot sew them together in a coherent way. (Hawthorne's Hester Prynne, by contrast, has a genius for sewing and embroidery.) She is radically not at home in all the customs in which she is born, no matter how hard she tries to accustom herself. She thus, with or without intention, mars what she does, and doing becomes undoing, just as "cousant" gives way to "décousait." Just how serious the implications of this unstitching activity are may be suggested by an abrupt authoritative assertion from one of Shakespeare's heroines, who is particularly notable for being innocent of the adultery that is basely imputed to her and for being a model of married fidelity, Imogen: "the breach of custom / Is breach of all" (*Cymbeline*, act 4, scene 2).

The other word to which I wish to return is *cou,* not as a root but as an independent word. In the first description of her person, Emma's neck is described in active terms—"Son cou sortait d'un col blanc." Her last voluntary act of motion *toward another person or thing* (her very last act is to ask for a look in a mirror, which is an act toward herself), involves another movement of the neck, but this time not, as it were, in repose but in an extreme of desperation. "The priest rose to take the crucifix. Reaching forward like one in thirst, she glued her lips to the body of the Man-God and laid upon it with all her failing strength the most mighty kiss of love she had ever given." ("Le prêtre se releva pour prendre le crucifix; alors elle allongea le cou comme quelqu'un qui a soif, et, collant ses lèvres sur le corps de l'Homme-Dieu, elle y déposa de toute sa force expirante le plus grand baiser d'amour qu'elle eût jamais donné.") The Man-God is the ultimate fusion in the Christian faith, as it is the sign of the confusion in Emma's life since the corporeal and the spiritual realms were, for her, blurred from the outset; a confusion she in part imbibed from the cross she kisses. But it is the stretching out of the neck that conveys so much of

Emma's plight, of the particular problem of her existence. At the risk of appearing to rehearse platitudes, let me emphasize some aspects of the role played by the neck in the human body. It is characteristically one of the three points of egress, or exits, at which the body leaves the clothes it wears, the other two being the hands and feet (these are also meticulously observed in Emma's actions). Feet and hands precipitate moving through (toward), and contact with (or manipulation of), the world, and are points at which the body visibly terminates. The neck in itself has no such specific skill (there are very few actions you *do* with your neck) but acts as the connecting link between the exposed head and the covered body; it is a tunnel containing the two-way traffic of words and nourishment, for it is in the neck that we start to swallow and to speak (thus it contains the throat, the vocal cords, the larynx, epiglottis, trachea, esophagus, etc.). It also allows the head its amazing flexibility, so that from birth we can track moving objects and locate differing sound sources. The head turns on the neck, and Emma is continually turning her head and, as we say, having her head turned. In particular, in this final stretching of her neck, she conveys the hopeless hungers, needs, and desires that have impelled her in her life, in her reachings out, turnings, extensions of her self.

If, perhaps somewhat fancifully, we considered the body as a complex word or unit of language, then we could say that the neck operates both as a word in itself and as a syllable in the more complex compound word of the body; by coming between the head and the chest and thus relating and separating them, it plays a crucial part in a larger unit of meaning. I have tried to suggest that something similar may be noted in Flaubert's text, where Emma's neck figures prominently in both her first appearance and her last, but where we also find the syllable *cou* appearing in a large number of longer words describing aspects of her activities and experiences—*coudre, couvrir, coutume, courbée, coûter, coups, couds, cour, coeur, couleuvre, courroie, couper,* etc. I am not trying to suggest any shared etymology, some secret hidden original meaning which we can track down to the source, hoping to experience in its presence an etymic epiphany. I am no more hoping to intimate that all these words can be traced back somehow to the meaning "neck" than one would try to see the different parts of the body as having some common source in the physical neck. My point is literally of the most superficial kind—for I only want to draw attention to a surface phenomenon, namely that the same three letters appear in this cluster of words, modified of course by the other letters they are associated with, just as when spoken the same, or a very similar, sound may be heard, modified of course by the other sounds immediately succeeding or preceding it. (Flaubert, I think, did something similar with *rou* and arguably with *tou,* but I will concentrate on *cou.*) These words, and the many others that could be cited, comprise what Saussure called an "associative series," and I must now quote from his work, *Course in General Linguistics.*

> In a language-state everything is based on relations. How do they function?
>
> Relations and differences between linguistic terms fall into two distinct groups, each of which generates a certain class of values. The opposition between the two classes gives a better understanding of the nature of each class. They correspond to two forms of our mental activity, both indispensable to the life of language.
>
> In discourse, on the one hand, words acquire relations based on the linear nature of language because they are chained together. This rules out the possibility of pronouncing two elements simultaneously. . . . The elements are arranged in sequence on the chain of speaking. Combinations supported by linearity are *syntagms.* . . . In the syntagm a term acquires its value only because it stands in opposition to everything that precedes or follows it, or to both.
>
> Outside discourse, on the other hand, words acquire relations of a different kind. Those that have something in common are associated in the memory, resulting in groups marked by diverse relations. . . .
>
> The coordinations formed outside discourse differ strikingly from those formed inside discourse. Those formed outside discourse are not supported by linearity. Their seat is in the brain; they are a part of the inner storehouse that makes up the language of each speaker. They are *associative relations.*
>
> The syntagmatic relation is *in praesentia.* It is based on two or more terms that occur in an effective series. Against this, the associative relation unites terms *in absentia* in a potential mnemonic series.

He then proceeds to expand on these different relations, and I want to quote from his remarks on "associative relations."

> Mental association creates other groups besides those based on the comparing of terms that have something in common; through its grasp of the nature of the relations that bind the

terms together, the mind creates as many associative series as
there are diverse relations. For instance, in *enseignement* "teach-
ing," *enseigner* "teach," *enseignons* "(we) teach," etc., one element, the radical, is common to every term; the same word
may occur in a different series formed around another common
element, the suffix (cf. *enseignement, armement, changement,* etc.);
or the association may spring from the analogy of the concepts
signified (*enseignement, instruction, apprentissage, education,* etc.);
or again, simply from the similarity of the sound-images (e.g.,
enseignement and *justement* "precisely").

At this point there is a footnote, to which I will return. Saussure's text
continues:

> Thus there is at times a double similarity of meaning and form,
> at times similarity only of form or of meaning. A word can al-
> ways evoke everything that can be associated with it in one
> way or another.
>
> Whereas a syntagm immediately suggests an order of succes-
> sion and a fixed number of elements, terms in an associative
> family occur neither in fixed numbers nor in a definite
> order. . . . We are unable to predict the number of words that
> the memory will suggest or the order in which they will ap-
> pear. A particular word is like the center of a constellation; it
> is the point of convergence of an indefinite number of co-
> ordinated terms.

In Flaubert's text *cou* operates as just such a word, it seems to me, and
it is the center of an indeterminate cluster of other words associated with
it in all the ways Saussure lists in the quotation, from identity of appearance with other syllables added, similarities and relatedness of meaning
and form, and simple similarity of the sound-images. I must now quote
from the footnote concerning this last kind of association, for once again
we find what amounts to almost a class attitude of contempt towards the
pun. "This last case [i.e., simple similarity of sound images] is rare and
can be classed as abnormal, for the mind naturally discards associations
that becloud the intelligibility of discourse. But its existence is proved by
a lower category of puns based on the ridiculous confusion that can result
from pure and simple homonymy. . . . This is distinct from the case
where an association, while fortuitous, is supported by a comparison of
ideas."

Again it should be pointed out that Flaubert can avail himself of both these ways of relating words, for his own purposes. But what is of particular interest here is Saussure's categorization of a certain kind of punning as abnormal on the grounds—and note the metaphor—that "the mind naturally discards associations that *becloud* the intelligibility of discourse." (My italics.) This follows quite logically from his whole idea of what language is, and again I want to quote from his own statements. "Psychologically our thought—apart from its expression in words—is only a shapeless and indistinct mass. Philosophers and linguists have always agreed in recognizing that without the help of signs we would be unable to make a clear-cut, consistent distinction between two ideas. Without language, thought is a vague, uncharted nebula. There are no preexisting ideas, and *nothing is distinct before the appearance of language.*" (My italics, and it is worth noting that although that statement might now be accepted as a truism, there is evidence to suggest that there is a good deal that is distinct before the appearance of language, and that initially language is a source of confusion and indistinction.) What Saussure stresses is that there are no "predelimited entities" either in the realm of ideas or of sounds. "Phonic substance is neither more fixed nor more rigid than thought; it is not a mold into which thought must of necessity fit but a plastic substance divided in turn into distinct parts to furnish the signifiers needed by thought." As he describes it, there is a mystery in what can only be called the ontology of language, or as he also calls it "the domain of articulations":

> Language works out its units while taking shape between two shapeless masses. Visualize the air in contact with a sheet of water; if the atmospheric pressure changes, the surface of the water will be broken up into a series of divisions, waves; the waves resemble the union or coupling of thought with phonic substance. . . .
>
> Linguistics then works in the borderland where the elements of sound and thought combine; *their combination produces a form, not a substance.*

The *source* of distinctions thus appears to be neither exclusively in sound nor in mind, but in their coming together in the linguistic unit ("The unit . . . is *a slice of sound which to the exclusion of everything that precedes and follows it in the spoken chain is the signifier of a certain concept.*") Since language is constantly transforming itself, changing, forgetting, substituting—"Language never stops interpreting and decomposing its units"—this brings into question the whole notion of stability of values (as indeed does his emphasis on the different degrees of arbitrariness operative in the formation or transformation of language). These *are* values but they are a function of difference—hence his stress on the importance of distinction as such, as a crucial phenomenon, and hence too his contempt for the low pun, which "clouds" the "intelligibility of discourse."

His remarks in this area are perhaps too familiar to require much more than allusion but I want to quote from one passage from the section entitled "The Sign Considered in Its Totality."

> Everything that has been said up to this point boils down to this: in language there are only differences. . . . Although both the signified and the signifier are purely differential and negative when considered separately [i.e., "their most precise characteristic is in being what the others are not"], their combination is a positive fact. . . .
>
> Any nascent difference will tend invariably to become significant but without always succeeding or being successful on the first trial. Conversely, any conceptual difference perceived by the mind seeks to find expression through a distinct signifier, and two ideas that are no longer distinct in the mind tend to merge into the same signifier.
>
> When we compare signs—positive terms—with each other, we can no longer speak of difference; the expression would not be fitting, for it applies only to the comparing of two sound-images, e.g., *father* and *mother,* or two ideas, e.g., the idea "father" the idea "mother"; two signs, each having a signified and signifier, are not different but only distinct. Between them there is only *opposition.* The entire mechanism of language . . . is based on oppositions of this kind and on the phonic and conceptual differences that they imply. . . .
>
> Applied to units, the principal of differentiation can be stated in this way: *the characteristics of the unit blend with the unit itself.* In language, as in any semiological system, whatever distinguishes one sign from the others constitutes it. *Difference makes character just as it makes value and the unit.* [The last italics are mine.]

The precise distinction between "difference" and "distinction" need not concern us here; I want rather to note Saussure's repeated stress on the fact that a word alone is nothing. "Each term present in the grammatical fact . . . consists of the interplay of a number of oppositions within the system. When isolated, neither *Nacht* nor *Nächte* is anything: thus everything is opposition." And again he reverts to the proposition "*language is a form and not a substance.*" Difference makes character and value, and language makes differences (information is, in Gregory Bateson's terms, "any difference which makes a difference in some later event"). It is the nonsubstantial form that introduces forms into the world of bodies and substances.

From the outset I have tried to suggest that Emma's problem is in part a crucial problem concerning distinctions and differences (hence the fog in her head), and that in turn this problem reflects a society losing its ability to maintain differences and distinctions (Rodolphe is only an emphasized example). What is it that "constitutes" Emma? She cannot find out, neither in marriage nor adultery nor in any other experience or in any terminology. The crisis of the meaning of marriage, which she experiences, is inextricably involved with, and indistinguishable from, a crisis in the language in and by which she is formed and rent. (It is notable and hardly incidental that Saussure's terms for discussing language overlap with those used in the realm of marriage—"associative family," "relations that bind," etc.) It is well established by now that in all societies marriage is a very important kind of language; it is perhaps worth reminding ourselves that the converse proposition also applies, so that language is a very important kind of marriage, a marriage between sound and concept, and by extension between speaker and listener. The marriage weakens in the case of writing, which, in Saussure's terms, creates "a purely fictitious unity"—"the superficial bond of writing is much easier to grasp than the only true bond, the bond of sound." This bond is the bond between sign and meaning, but it applies just as well to the bond between writer and reader. This is no place to attempt any consideration of a topic as all-embracing as the differences between speaking and writing. My point, a more limited one, is that Flaubert's whole book makes us aware in a new way that the crisis in marriage is also, and not by metaphor but by identity, a crisis in language. To put it very simply, we may recognize four stages in Emma's life: singleness or "daughterhood," marriage, adultery, death (this is indeed a stage or period, for it does not come as an abrupt, sudden event). These may be paralleled by four stages in the life of language (as depicted in the book): the prelingual stage (singleness); a period when the interplay and relationship of differences *seems* stable and binding, during which time meaning is agreed on and nonproblematical (marriage); a period marked by an accelerating "decomposition" and reinterpretation of "units" (adultery); and the death of this particular phase of language as another one emerges to take its place (Emma's death and the total, ubiquitous triumph of Homais at the end of the book). Emma is caught between, not two languages, but two ways of using language, two different modes of constituting "meaning." Her giddiness and tottering, her confused and desperate searching—in short, the fog in her head—can be attributed to a large extent to her vague and hopeless yearning for a kind of meaning that the existing language into which she is born seems to promise (with its religious and romantic vocabularies, etc.), but that in fact it can no longer deliver or bestow. Before Emma broke her word to Charles, language had broken its word to her. Before Emma committed adultery, meanings had slipped bonds and moved into other beds or disappeared entirely. And when she dies, the death agonies of her final disintegration are the physical registration of the disintegration of an old and superseded kind of language. They are both a long time dying, but by the end they are both utterly dead. Which is, to reiterate a crucial point, why Flaubert abandons the *nous* with which he started his book. All the bonds and ties and contracts and relationships have effectively been broken or are dissolved. "The breach of custom/ Is breach of all." Imogen's awesomely succinct formulation applies equally to the marriage that is language and the language that is marriage. Flaubert's book is a study of all those nonlegalized divorces that result from that loss of the sense of difference that makes breaches of custom and all adulterations of relationships possible.

Saussure designated two relationships in a language state, one inside discourse and the other outside. The syntagmatic relationship fixes words in chains; it is based on a linear combination and is characterized by an order of succession and a fixed number of elements. It is a definite order and the constituent parts take on their meaning from their place in the chain. Given this definition, it is hardly inappropriate to regard marriage as a syntagmatic relationship. This is the relationship in discourse in which words are chained together. It is *in praesentia*. The associative relations are unlimited, unfixed, in no definite order, unpredictable, diverse, the convergence of an indefinite number of coordinated terms, terms coordinated not according to the grammatical rules that govern the syntagmatic order, but by a multiplicity of diverse habits of association (similarity of sound, construction, meaning, connotation, etc.). It is a relationship outside discourse and is *in absentia*. Within it, many words come together in unpredictable combinations—such as *cou, coudre, courvrir, coutume, couleuvre, courroie, couper*, etc., etc.—but none of them are chained together in a fixed relationship. This is the equivalent of the realm where adulterous relationships obtain. Inasmuch as we all think in associative relations and speak in syntagms, then we may all be said to participate in these marital/adulterous aspects of language, the condition of being both absent and present, both inside and outside discourse at the same time. Again we must recognize that Emma's is not a unique but an exemplary case. She is inserted into a syntagmatic relationship, but her whole being tends to think and feel in (increasingly confused) associative constellations. Both of these modes of establishing relations are inherent in the language, indeed in *la condition lin-guistique*. They need not necessarily come into conflict or engender it, but the potential for doing so is always there, and in the figure of Emma Bovary, Flaubert concentrates on just that latent potentiality. Syntagmatic and associative relations are confused and confounded, thus precipitating confoundings in all aspects of Emma's existence: "the appetites of the flesh, the craving for money, the melancholy of passion, all blended together in one general misery" ("les appétits de la chair, les convoitises d'argent et les mélancolies de la passion, tout se confondit dans une même souffrance"). Flaubert's opening description of Charles Bovary's cap depicts it as an associative series or set of relationships gone berserk, not a constellation or coordination, but a chaos. As Charles is ac-costumed so is he ac-customed, and that cap bespeaks a crisis in language in which recognizable families or relationships are being replaced by jumbles of signs that not only make no sense but actively serve to destroy it. (Needless to say, a crisis in language is inseparable from a crisis in customs!) In the particular kind of disintegration and decomposition of language that Flaubert localizes in Emma's consciousness and on her tongue, by a hopeless and lethal paradox the differences that should make the difference instead break the difference, and work to the disestablishment of distinctions (thus when Emma is described both "tout en cousant" and "décousait," she is only doing what language is doing to her). More clearly than ever, Flaubert's careful arrangement of words, maintaining a constant hyperconsciousness of all their differences and similarities, makes us aware to just what an extent the fog in Emma Bovary's head is ultimately language—language in a critical state of malaise that indeed turns out to be fatal. That fog is a sign of the irresolvable difficulty of participating in a pleonastic proliferation of terms that is then compounded by the obligatory but illusory and unstable distinctions imposed by marriage, which, for Emma, confuses where it is supposed to clarify and separates where it joins.

For a Restricted Thematics:
Writing, Speech,
and Difference in *Madame Bovary*

Naomi Schor

It is time to say out loud what has been whispered for some time: thematic criticism, which was given a first-class funeral a few years ago, is not dead. Like a repressed desire that insists on returning to consciousness, like a guilty pleasure that resists all threat of castration, thematic criticism is coming out from the shadows. This new thematic criticism is not, however, a nostalgic textual practice, a "retro" criticism, a regression to the styles (of reading) of the 1950s. Just as hyperrealism in painting is a return to the figurative passed through a minimalist grid, neothematism is a thematism passed through the filter of structuralist criticism. One could even argue that a certain structuralism, namely structural semantics, was in fact never anything but recuperation of thematism, a structuralist neothematism.

But it is not our purpose to study the persistence of thematics; the point is not, within the narrow framework of our study, to anticipate a history of contemporary criticism which is yet to be written. Rather it is a question of opening an inquiry into the continuity that links thematics, structural semantics, and even "poststructuralism." This very undertaking, this implicit valorization of continuity, is precisely what to our eyes constitutes thematics' characteristic, distinctive feature: I shall term thematic all textual practices that suffer from what might be called, in the manner of Bachelard, an Ariadne complex, all readings that cling to the Ariadne's thread ("fil conducteur"), whether it be the "synonymic chains"

From *The Future of Difference,* edited by Hester Eisenstein and Alice Jardine. © 1980 by Naomi Schor. G. K. Hall, 1980. This essay was translated by Harriet Stone.

of Barthes, the "chain of supplements" of Derrida, or the "series" of Deleuze. Be it vertical, horizontal, or transversal, the Ariadne's thread haunts
the texts of Barthes, Derrida, and Deleuze, not in the typically structuralist
form—that is, metalinguistic—of the Greimasian isotope, but in a poetic
form: the thread ("fil") has become an extended metaphor. As Deleuze's
"spider web," Barthes's "braid," and Derrida's "texture" indicate, the relationship between the "textual" and the "textile" is on its way to becoming one of the obsessive metaphors of current criticism. How are we to
explain this obsession common to thinkers otherwise so different? One seductive hypothesis is that they all draw from the same source, namely
Proust's metaphoric repertory. The following quotations from Richard
(on Proust), Derrida (on Plato), and Barthes (on the pleasure of the text)
substantiate this notion:

> Thematization thus clearly resembles weaving. The interweav-
> ing of all thematic series assumes in the Proustian daydream the
> form of a net in which the matter of the work is caught, or that
> of a network, both innervational and cybernetic, that enables us
> to circulate in it from link to link, knot to knot, "star" to
> "star" with the utmost freedom; because "between the least sig-
> nificant point in our past and all the others there exists a rich
> network of memories offering a plethora of communications."
>
> (*Proust et le monde sensible*)

> The dissimulation of the woven texture can in any case take
> centuries to undo its web: a web that envelops a web, undoing
> the web for centuries; reconstituting it too as an organism, in-
> definitely regenerating its own tissue behind the cutting trace,
> the decision of each reading. There is always a surprise in store
> for the anatomy or physiology of a critique that might think it
> had mastered the game, surveyed all the threads at once, a cri-
> tique that deludes itself too, in wanting to look at the text with-
> out touching it, without laying a hand on the "object," without
> risking—which is the sole chance of entering into the game by
> getting a few fingers caught—the addition of some new thread.
> Adding, here, is nothing other than giving to read. One must
> manage to think this out: that it is not a question of embroider-
> ing upon a text, unless one considers that to know how to em-
> broider is still to take heed to follow the given thread. That is,
> if you follow me, the hidden thread."
>
> ("Plato's Pharmacy," in *Dissemination*)

While taking the opposite view from Derrida insofar as hidden meaning is concerned, Barthes adopts his textile metaphor; Derrida's *istos* becomes Barthes's *hyphos*:

> *Text* means *Tissue;* but whereas hitherto we have always taken this tissue as a product, a ready-made veil, behind which lies, more or less hidden, meaning (truth), we are now emphasizing, in the tissue, the generative idea that the text is made, is worked out in a perpetual interweaving; lost in this tissue—this texture—the subject makes himself, like a spider dissolving in the constructive secretions of its web. Were we fond of neologism, we might define the theory of the text as an *hyphology* (*hyphos* is the tissue and the spider's web).
>
> (*The Pleasure of the Text*)

The metaphors that these authors weave again and again are extremely significant, since according to Freud the only contribution of women "to the discoveries and inventions in the history of civilization" is a "technique," "that of plaiting and weaving." The thread unraveled by Ariadne, cut by the Fates, woven by Penelope, is a peculiarly feminine attribute, a metonym for femininity. There is thus cause to speculate about the relations (necessarily hypothetical at the current stage of our knowledge) between a thematic reading and a feminine reading, by which I certainly do not mean that reading practiced uniquely by women. If my hypothesis concerning the femininity of thematism were justified, this would explain its culpabilization on the one hand and, paradoxically, its masculine recuperation on the other. This hypothesis presupposes a question: does reading have a sex? And this question in turn brings up another: does writing have a sex? It is, as we will attempt to demonstrate, precisely this question of the sex of writing that underlies *Madame Bovary*. We can no longer read *Madame Bovary* outside of the "sexual problematic" that Sartre analyzed in its author (in *The Family Idiot*), but we must no longer separate the sexual problematic from the scriptural problematic, as did Baudelaire, who was the first to qualify Emma Bovary as a "strange androgynous creature."

Let us note at the close, in order to weave the many threads of our introduction, that there exists in *Madame Bovary* the description of an object which can be readily inscribed in the line of thought that we have just evoked. I am referring to the green silk cigar-case that Charles picks up when leaving la Vaubyessard and that Emma so preciously keeps. Read, or reread, in light of the preceding remarks, this passage seems to assume a new meaning: the green silk cigar-case becomes the emblem of the imbrication of weaving, the text, and femininity. *Madame Bovary* thus contains not only an objective correlative of its production, but a protocol for its interpretation as well:

> It had been embroidered on some rosewood frame, a pretty piece of furniture, hidden from all eyes, that had occupied many hours, and over which had fallen the soft curls of the pensive worker. A breath of love had passed over the stitches on the canvas; each prick of the needle had fixed there a hope or a memory, and all those interwoven threads of silk were but the continued extension of the same silent passion.

To conclude these prolegomena, I would like to put to the test a new thematics that I propose to call a "restricted thematics" because, if the definition of the field of possible themes must henceforth answer to the call for literary specificity, the reciprocal play of speech and writing will replace the time/space paradigm privileged since Proust, with speech occupying the field of time, and writing inscribed in that of space. Unlike the "general" thematic reading which always tends toward "an infinite reading" (Richard), which exists, that is, in an anamorphous relationship with the text, restricted thematics would be the equivalent of an anastomosis, sectioning the text in order to bring together binary opposites (on the semantic plane), doubles (on the actantial plane), and repeated sequences (on the evenemential plane).

> *En somme, cette femme est vraiment grande, elle est surtout pitoyable, et malgré la dureté systématique de l'auteur, qui a fait tous ses efforts pour être absent de son oeuvre et pour jouer la fonction d'un monteur de marionnettes, toutes les femmes intellectuelles lui sauront gré d'avoir élevé la femelle à une si haute puissance, si loin de l'animal pur et si près de l'homme idéal.*
>
> (Baudelaire)

As a starting-point for our reflection, let us recall René Girard's statement concerning Flaubert's "grotesque antithesis":

> As Flaubert's novelistic genius ripens his oppositions become more futile; the identity of the contraries is drawn more clearly.
>
> (*Deceit, Desire and the Novel*)

If—as we are firmly convinced—this breakdown of opposites is manifest at all levels of the Flaubertian text and along its entire diachronic course, how does it apply to the writing/speech opposition, explicitly

thematized by Flaubert in *Sentimental Education,* during a conversation between Frédéric and Madame Arnoux: "She admired orators; he preferred
a writer's fame." Does this orators/writers opposition also participate in
the obsessional tyranny of the identity of the contraries, in this system of
growing in–differentiation?

The speech axis permits a first division of the characters in *Madame
Bovary* into two large categories: those who are adept at speaking, such as
Rodolphe and Homais, and those who are not, such as Charles and
Emma. But the insufficiency of this first distribution is instantly apparent
since certain characters adept at speaking are not good listeners. The
speech axis must be subordinated to the communication axis, a bipolar
axis with at one end an encoder/emitter, at the other a decoder/receiver.
Depending on whether or not a character exhibits the aptitudes for encoding and decoding, we can forsee four combinations:

(1) encoding + (2) encoding − (3) encoding + (4) encoding −
    decoding +   decoding −   decoding −   decoding +

If we examine the characters named above in light of these *roles,* certain
aspects of the speech problematic in *Madame Bovary* emerge.

From his first appearance, Charles reveals himself to be an impotent
speaker:

> The new boy then took a supreme resolution, opened an inor-
> dinately large mouth, and shouted at the top of his voice as if
> calling someone, the word "Charbovari."

Incapable of articulating the syllables of his name, Charles can but repeat
the words of others:

> Charles's conversation was commonplace as a street pavement,
> and every one's ideas trooped through it in their everyday garb,
> without exciting emotion, laughter, or thought.

What distinguishes Charles's conversation from that of the glib speaker is
not so much its painful banality, but its neutrality. His is an inefficient
speech, lacking resonance, a speech in which nothing is transmitted from
the enunciator to his interlocutor. Nevertheless, it must be noted that this
"zero" on the encoding plane will have a great word, his last:

> He even made a phrase ("un grand mot"), the only one he'd
> ever made:
>   "Fate willed it this way."

The effect of this grandiloquent sentence is, however, doubly subverted by its receptor, Rodolphe:

> Rodolphe, who had been the agent of this fate, thought him very meek for a man in his situation, comic even and slightly despicable.

First irony: the receptor is, in fact, the encoder. It is Rodolphe who was the first to put the word "fate" into circulation in the novel when he composed his letter breaking with Emma:

> Why were you so beautiful? Is it my fault? God, no! only fate is to blame!
> "That's a word that always helps," he said to himself.

And Charles reads this letter. As we will see below, once launched, this word will continually reappear. In using it in talking to Rodolphe, Charles only completes the series, closes the circuit: Rodolphe→Emma→Charles →Rodolphe. Second irony: the original encoder (the "voluntary deceiver" [Claude Brémont, *Logique du récit*]), presents himself as judge and condemns his imitator (his involuntary dupe). Flaubert thus puts the parrot and the hypocrite back to back.

With Charles the inability to encode goes along with an inability to decode which makes him unable to understand Emma. For Emma, speaking to Charles is a last resort:

> At other times, she told him what she had been reading, some passage in a novel, a new play, or an anecdote from high society found in a newspaper story; for, after all, Charles was someone to talk to, an ever-open ear, an ever-ready approbation. She even confided many a thing to her greyhound! She would have done so to the logs in the fireplace or to the pendulum of the clock.

Charles's qualifications as a listener are minimal; they can be reduced to the possession of an ear and the promise of his ever-identical reaction. The equivalence established among Charles, the greyhound, the logs, and the pendulum says a great deal about his inability to decode, for the progression from the animate to the inanimate, the choice of the logs and the pendulum in the domestic code, with their semes of hardness (hence the figurative meaning of "bûche" [log]: "stupid person") and mechanicity, confirms Charles's nullity: he actualizes combination no. 2, which is doubly negative.

Initially, Rodolphe seems gifted with all the faculties that Charles lacks. This is not to say that his discourse is more "original" than Charles's, but that he draws from the same dictionary of received ideas as Emma: he speaks her language. The juxtaposition in the oft-commented-upon chapter of the agricultural fair of Rodolphe's conventional seduction of Emma and the functionaries' set speech serves only to underscore the parallelism of the two discourses: opposed on the spatial (vertical) axis, Rodolphe and the two orators echo each other on the speech axis, as the intersection of the two discourses indicates. The only difference between Rodolphe's speech and that of Charles is that Rodolphe's acts upon Emma; it evokes dreams, it becomes action, love.

A clever encoder, Rodolphe is also a cunning decoder of corporeal semiology: he is a diagnostician of great talent:

> Monsieur Roldophe Boulanger was thirty-four; he combined brutality of temperament with a shrewd judgment, having had much experience with women and being something of a connoisseur. This one had seemed pretty to him; so he kept dreaming about her and her husband.
>
> "I think he is very stupid. She must be tired of him, no doubt. *He has dirty nails, and hasn't shaved for three days.*" (my italics)

But it is precisely that which enables him to decode this *clue,* namely his experience, that prevents him from decoding Emma's oral messages. Having spent his life repeating, indeed perfecting, an invariable scenario whose only variant is the partner, Rodolphe cannot go beyond clichés, ready-made formulas. Everything happens as if Rodolphe's decoding mechanism were programmed to function only with information that has already been received. We find in Rodolphe the same "linguistic deafness" that Genette analyzes in certain Proustian characters who, he remarks, only hear what they can or want to hear, that is, in the extreme, what they can or want to say ("Proust et le langage indirect," in *Figures 2*). Rodolphe's decoding of Charles's speech (see above) exemplifies this form of listening by projection. Emma's case is, however, far more complex:

> He had so often heard these things said that they did not strike *him* as original. Emma was like all his mistresses; and the charm of novelty, gradually falling away like a garment, laid bare the eternal monotony of passion, that has always the same shape and the same language. He was unable to see, this man so full

of experience, the variety of feelings hidden within the same expressions. Since libertine or venal lips had murmured similar
phrases, he only faintly believed in the candor of Emma's; he
thought one should be aware of exaggerated declarations which
only serve to cloak a tepid love; *as though* the abundance of
one's soul did not sometimes overflow with empty metaphors,
since no one ever has been able to give the exact measure of his
needs, his concepts, or his sorrows. The human tongue is like
a cracked cauldron on which we beat out the tunes to set a bear
dancing when we would make the stars weep with our melo-
dies. (my italics)

The increased intervention of the narrator from the "him" of disassocia-
tion (indirect intervention) to the "as though" of judgment (direct intervention) translates the importance that Flaubert attaches to this passage, in
which he puts forth his speech problematic. In effect, this passage does no
more than reiterate an invariant opposition: unique feelings versus common speech. In other words: how does one communicate difference by
means of sameness, how does one give an individual charge to words used
by all? With Flaubert the renewal of the cliché is not so much a matter of
style as metaphysics, for, on a purely linguistic plane, there is in his work
as a constant inspiration by the cliché, an aspiration by the received idea.
Thus in *Sentimental Education* the cliché favors more than it prevents the
communication of passionate feelings: "He . . . poured out his love more
freely through the medium of commonplaces." But what the cliché cannot
communicate is unicity. Two presuppositions underlie this passage: first,
there is a "dissimilarity of feelings," original feelings, unique essence; second, in an ideal system of speech there is a total adequation of the word
and the psychic signified. Flaubert's oral ideal is, to use Genette's expression, nothing but a new "avatar of cratylism" (*Mimologiques Voyage en Cra-
tylic*), which is hardly surprising in this avowed Platonist.

    Madame Bovary tests the romantic notions of exceptionality and ineffa-
bility, for the destiny of the romantic hero is bound up with a theory of
speech. The "double intervention" (Victor Brombert, *Flaubert par lui-
même*) noted above translates the doubling of the narrative sequence; we
could adopt here the writer/novelist distinction proposed by Marcel Muller
to account for two of the seven voices in *Remembrance of Things Past* (*Les
Voix narratives dans* La Recherche du temps perdu), attributing to the
"writer" Rodolphe's point of view, and to the "novelist" Emma's. To as-
sign Rodolphe's decoding a minus sign—Rodolphe would actualize combi-

nation no. 3—amounts to espousing the cause of the novelist, who supports Emma's essential superiority/difference, betrayed not only by the inferiority of those who surround her, but also by speech, which is not up to her level. René Girard, it should be noted here, adopts the point of view of the writer, indirectly justifying Rodolphe: "the opposition between Emma and Charles, and between Emma and the citizens of Yonville is essential only in Emma's mind."

If, however, we follow the thread of the thematic paradigm speech/ writing, we find that the structuring opposition of the novel is neither Emma versus Rodolphe nor Emma versus Charles (nor is it the commonplace of traditional criticism, Homais versus Bournisien); the privileged doublet is none other than Emma versus Homais, a fundamental opposition half-expressed, half-concealed by their names, which should be read "Femm(a) versus Hom(ais)"—*Femme* (Woman) versus *Homme* (Man). This reading consists of remedying Emma's lack by restoring her truncated "F" to her, and of cutting off Homais's supplement by putting his adjunctive suffix in parentheses. How can one fail to see in the operations to which Flaubert subjected the terms of sexual opposition to generate the characters' names, the equivalent of castration on the plane of the signifier? We could thus term the castration axis the arch-axis, the principal axis that subordinates all the other semantic axes of the novel.

Opposed to Emma's inability to find the words necessary to express her thoughts (one of the corollaries of the cratylian theory being that thoughts/feelings *precede* speech) is the always reiterated adequation of the pharmacist's thoughts and words:

> Perhaps she would have liked to confide all these things to some one. But how tell an undefinable uneasiness, changing as the clouds, unstable as the winds? Words failed her and, by the same token, the opportunity, the courage.

> "What a dreadful catastrophe!" exclaimed the pharmacist, who always found expressions that filled all imaginable circumstances.

Emma's incapacity, let us note, is intermittent; her cyclothymia is also a pathology of speech:

> On certain days she chattered with feverish profusion, and this overexcitement was suddenly followed by a state of torpor, in which she remained without speaking, without moving.

This alternate encoding can be represented as follows:

Emma: encoding + / −

Nevertheless, on the speech-encoding plane, Homais is the undisputed winner. Of all the characters in the novel, he is the only one to work tirelessly at his expression. For him talking is both a delight (*jouissance*) ("for the pharmacist much enjoyed pronouncing the word 'doctor,' as if addressing another by it reflected on himself some of the grandeur of the title," and an art ("Homais had meditated at length over his speech; he had rounded, polished it, given it the proper cadence; it was a masterpiece of prudence and transitions, of subtle turns and delicacy"). Unlike Rodolphe, Homais does not speak a stilted language, but takes pleasure in hearing and reproducing new thoughts, stylish expressions. Thus we see him, in the course of a conversation with Léon, reveal his extraordinary mimetic gifts, speaking "Parislang":

> He even used slang to impress [. . .] the "bourgeois," saying "flip," "cool," "sweet," "neat-o," and "I must break it up," for "I must leave."

If Rodolphe is a smooth talker, if he dexterously manages the code of the vile seducer, Homais has a gift for *languages* (Latin, English, slang) that he handles with the love of a savant, an expert in transcoding.

But if on the communication axis Homais wins out over Emma, who, it must be remembered, does not shine as a decoder, allowing herself to be easily duped by the clichés that Rodolphe reels off to her both before and after their affair ("It was the first time Emma had heard such words addressed to her, and her pride unfolded languidly in the warmth of this language, like someone stretching in a hot bath"; "She yielded to his words"), when one turns to that delayed communication, writing, the balance of forces is equalized. Certain readers, unaware of Emma's scriptural activities, will perhaps be surprised at this affirmation. It is, however, in the area of writing that the Emma/Homais rivalry turns out to be the most violent; it is to the extent that they practice two different forms of writing that their sexual opposition becomes significant. The medal that motivates Homais and whose reception closes the novel—"He has just been given the cross of the Legion of Honor"—is destined to crown his writings, which are numerous. He is the classic pedant scribbler, having published " 'at my expense, numerous work of public usefulness, such as' (and he recalled his pamphlet entitled, *On Cider, Its Manufacture and Effects,* besides observations on the wooly aphis that he had sent to the Academy; his volume of statistics, and down to his pharmaceutical thesis)." Compared to this journalistic logorrhea, what has Emma published? Nothing, but she does write. What, to my knowledge, has escaped critical notice is the thematic and structural relationship between *Madame Bovary* and the first *Education*: the Emma/Homais couple is a new avatar of the Jules/Henry couple. Even those who have taken literally the famous exclamation *"Madame Bovary, c'est moi"* have bypassed the essential, the too-evident, in their concern for the anecdotal similarities between Emma and Gustave. Emma is also the portrait of an artist, but of the artist as a young woman, and it is this difference, this bold representation of the writer as a woman which disconcerts, which misleads, and which, for these reasons, must be examined.

Emma's search for love's passion is doubly motivated by literature. First there is "external mediation" (Girard), the desire to transform the (dead) letters that she has read into lived experience, to coincide with literary models:

> And Emma tried to find out what one meant exactly in life by the words *bliss, passion, ecstasy,* that had seemed to her so beautiful in books.

When she becomes Rodolphe's mistress, this much longed-for identification seems to be realized; Emma progresses from the passive status of a reader to the active status of a heroine:

> Then she recalled the heroines of the books that she had read. . . . She became herself, as it were, an actual part of these lyrical imaginings; at long last, as she saw herself among those lovers she had so envied, she fulfilled the love-dream of her youth.

Finally, with Léon she attains her goal: from a heroine-for-herself she is transformed into a heroine-for-others: "She was the mistress of all the novels, the heroine of all the dramas, the vague 'she' of all the volumes of verse."

But this first love-letters link conceals another of prime importance to our study: Emma seeks a lover not only to become a novelistic character, but especially to become an author. When, in the early stage of her marriage, Emma settles in to wait for "something to happen," she outfits herself in advance with a writer's tools:

> She had bought herself a blotter, writing-case, pen-holder, and
> envelopes although *she had no one to write to*. (my italics)

What Emma lacks is not a lover, but a receiver ("destinaire"), and what
she desires through this receiver-pretext for writing is literary fame. To
convince oneself of this, one need only compare the above quotation with
another seemingly innocent remark which follows one page later. Emma
wants Charles to become a great doctor because:

> She would have wished this name of Bovary, which was hers,
> to be illustrious, to see it displayed at the booksellers', repeated
> in the newspapers, known to all France.

By bringing together these two segments of the same sentence, of the
same phantasm, we witness the emergence of Emma's profound ambition:
to be a famous novelist. Why then is this wish expressed on the one hand
by an intermediary, projected onto Charles, and on the other hand oc-
culted by the separation of the means (writing instruments) from the end
(to be famous)? This repression, this censure, results from Emma's sex.
What she envies in a man is not so much the possibility of traveling, but
the possibility of writing; what she lacks in order to write are neither
words nor pen, but a phallus.

Imbued with eighteenth-century literature, Emma cannot conceive of
a literary production other than a novel by letters, and the taking of a lover
is the necessary condition for this form of writing. Once she becomes Ro-
dophe's mistress, Emma begins her epistolary novel. Rodolphe serves as
both her initiator and her receiver:

> From that day on they wrote to one another regularly every
> evening. Emma placed her letter at the end of the garden, by
> the river, in a crack of the wall. Rodolphe came to fetch it, and
> put another in its place that she always accused of being too
> short.

This little game of hide-and-seek inaugurates Emma's apprenticeship,
which will go through three stages, the first of which is marked by the
persistence of the illusion of communication. Rather than denounce this
illusion, Emma brings to correspondence all those desires unsatisfied by
conversation, continuing to valorize *exchange,* clinging to the double role
of sender/receiver that defines the interlocutor. Thus Emma complains of
the brevity of Rodolphe's letters; thus she demands verses from Léon:

> She asked him for some verses—some verses "for herself," a
> "love poem" in honor of her.

If initially Emma writes to receive letters, to take pleasure in the communication forbidden, impossible on the speech plane, writing subsequently becomes the adjuvant of a "waning passion" in the manner of an aphrodisiac:

> In the letters that Emma wrote him she spoke of flowers, poetry, the moon and the stars, naive resources of a waning passion striving to keep itself alive by all external aids.

It is only during the third stage when the receiver-lover has been demystified, unmasked as the double of her husband—"Emma found again in adultery all the platitudes of marriage" (an excellent example of the identity of opposites!)—that Emma must yield to the evidence: she no longer loves Léon, but she continues more and more to love to write. It is only at this stage that Emma fully assumes her role as writer:

> She blamed Léon for her disappointed hopes, as if he had betrayed her. . . .
>
> She none the less went on writing him love letters in keeping with the notion that a woman must write to her lover.
>
> But while writing to him, it was another man she saw, a phantom fashioned out of her most ardent memories, of her favorite books, her strongest desires, and at last he became so real, so tangible, that her heart beat wildly in awe and admiration, though unable to see him distinctly, for, like a god, he was hidden beneath the abundance of his attributes. . . . she felt him near her; he was coming and would ravish her entire being in a kiss. Then she would fall back to earth again shattered; for these vague ecstasies of imaginary love would exhaust her more than the wildest orgies.

The "but" signals the passage from one stage to another, the final subordination of love to writing, the metamorphosis of writing dictated by conventions into writing that flows from the heart. The latter writing is diametrically opposed to conversation-communication in that it presupposes the absence of a receiver, compensates for a lack, thereby embracing emptiness. As Freud demonstrates in *The Poet and Daydreaming,* the fictive character, like this composite being who is sketched by Emma's pen, is the product of all the unsatisfied desires of its creator. Transcoded into psychoanalytic terminology, the "phantom" that Emma perceives is a phantasm. Moreover, writing, such as Emma practices it (such as Flaubert practiced it), is a solitary pleasure; the phantasmic scene is seduction. The pleasure that Emma experiences in rewriting Léon, in giving herself a lover three times hyperbolic, is intensely erotic.

To write is to leave the prey for the shadow, and, in the end, writing is to become the shadow itself; the author-phantom must succeed the character-phantom. Thus, just before swallowing the arsenic, Emma appears to Justin "majestic as a phantom." The apprenticeship of the heroine-artist can lead only to death, but to an exemplary death, because suicide generates language. In the novel to die a natural death (*belle mort*) is to commit suicide, because suicide is the very act that links the coming to writing with the renunciation of life. Like Madame de Tourvel, like Julie, Emma does not die without having written a last letter: "She sat down at her writing-table and wrote a letter, which she sealed slowly, adding the date and the hour." Of this letter we know only the first words: " 'Let no one be blamed . . .' " The fragmentary state of this letter is highly significant, because the gap created by the ellipsis leaves forever unanswered the essential question: in this ultimate letter, *ultima verba*, does Emma complete the final stages of her apprenticeship, does she succeed in inventing for herself a writing that goes beyond clichés, beyond the romantic lies that they carry with them? The first words are only a (negative) repetition of Rodolphe's words, tending to invalidate any hypothesis of last-minute literary conversion. This letter immediately evokes the imitative circuit. If, in the letter that Charles composes right after Emma's death, we find both thematic (novelistic ideas) and stylistic (use of the imperative: " 'Let no one try to overrule me' ") echoes of Emma's previous letters, we are struck, too, by the firmness of expression resulting from a very bold use of asyndeton. In fact, one could cite this passage as an example of the Flaubertian enunciation which, according to Barthes's formula, is seized by "a generalized asyndeton":

> I wish her to be buried in her wedding dress, with white shoes, and a wreath. Her hair is to be spread out over her shoulders. Three coffins, one oak, one mahogany, one of lead. Let no one try to overrule me; I shall have the strength to resist him. She is to be covered with a large piece of green velvet. This is my wish; see that it is done.

Is this writing a personal find of Charles's, whose writing up to this point vied in ineptitude with his speech (note the fifteen drafts that he writes to have Dr. Larivière come *before* Emma's death), or can one see in it the pale reflection, traces of Emma's last letter?

In the Flaubertian novelistic universe, in which substitution chains organize the narrative, nothing is less evident than the principles of closure that govern this neurotic serialization. Since in Emma's mind the Viscount

= Léon = Rodolphe, what prevents her from continuing indefinitely this substitution of one lover for another? In theory the series is open-ended; the resources of a substantial rhetoric and logic are inexhaustible. In effect, Emma's death is not synchronic with the exhaustion of the narrative because, after her death, she is replaced by other characters: formerly the *subject* of substitution, she becomes its *object*. Thus Félicité, her maid, wears her dresses: "[she] was about her former mistress's height and often, on seeing her from behind, Charles thought she had come back"; and Charles begins to imitate her.

> To please her, as if she were still living, he adopted her taste, her ideas; he bought patent leather boots and took to wearing white cravats. He waxed his moustache and, just like her, signed promissory notes.

But, on the actantial plane, on the plane of the novel's structuring opposition, Emma/Homais, Emma is succeeded by the blind man, a Beckettian character whose *symbolic* value has for a long time preoccupied the critics and whose function still remains to be pinpointed. According to our reading, his function is above all heuristic: whereas the opposition between Emma and Homais is implicit, concealed by anagrams, that between the blind man and Homais is explicit, manifest on the evenemential plane.

The blind man's doubling of Emma is prepared a long time in advance: from his first appearance the blind man finds in Emma a listener; his melancholic song evokes an echo in Emma's mind; later she gives him her last five-franc coin (see in this scene the opposition: Emma's excessive generosity versus Homais's excessive greed; by her *gift,* Emma is united with the blind man against Homais). Finally, on her deathbed, Emma hears the blind man, believes she sees him, and pronounces her last words: " 'The blind man!' " The seme common to Emma and the blind man is monstrosity, physical in the one, moral in the other. It is precisely the blind man's monstrosity that brings upon him Homais's hostility: Homais would like to cure the blind man, that is, reduce his difference, "normalize" him. The blind man/Homais sequence only repeats the clubfoot/Homais sequence; in both cases the science preached by the pharmacist is never anything but the means of replacing heterogeneity with homogeneity, thereby earning the gratitude and esteem of his clients. Nevertheless, unlike the crippled clubfoot, the blind-man-ever-blind flouts Homais, publicly exhibiting the wounds that the pharmacist's recommendations and pomades could not cure. Homais, unable to silence this embarrassing witness to the inefficacy of his speech, begins to pursue him through writing;

a fierce fight ensues between the garrulous blind man and the prolix pharmacist:

> He managed so well that the fellow was locked up. But he was released. He began again, and so did Homais. It was a struggle. Homais won out, for his foe was condemned to lifelong confinement in an asylum.

The superimposition of the Emma/Homais // blind man/Homais rivalries reveal within writing the same opposition that we detected above at the center of speech: efficacy versus inefficacy. We can thus posit the following equivalence:

$$\frac{\text{Efficacy}}{\text{Inefficacy}} \simeq \frac{\text{Rodolphe's speech}}{\text{Charles's speech}} \simeq \frac{\text{Homais's writing}}{\text{Emma's writing}}$$

While Emma's writing remains, so to speak, a dead letter, transforming nothing, producing no impact on the external world, Homais's writing is able to exile if not kill, and becomes a means of social advancement.

Moreoever, this superimposition permits the disengagement of an attribute, an invariant qualification of the *victim:* the victim, woman or blind man, is a being who lacks an essential organ, in fact, as Freud repeats at several points, the same organ, since according to his theory blindness = castration. The victim's final failure is inscribed in his/her body; Emma's monstrosity is physical as much as it is moral. The blind man's doubling of Emma punctuates the text, assures it readability: woman, this "defective" monster (*"monstre à la manque"*), is the privileged figure of the writer, and especially of the writer Flaubert, a "failed girl" (*"fille manquée"*) according to Sartre's thesis. It would, moreover, be easy to demonstrate that Emma's writing apprenticeship is consistent with an attempt to change sex, to reverse castration. The refusal of femininity, the temptation of virility, are not given once and for all from the beginning; before going that route, Emma will try to follow the path of integration, to accept the feminine destiny that Freud charts for the "normal" woman: marriage and maternity. But, just as marriage ends in failure, Charles being unable to succeed *in Emma's place,* motherhood ends in disappointment: George, the phantasmic phallic-son, turns out to be only Berthe, a child worthy of Charles. Thus, much before Freud, Flaubert well understood that in order for maternity to fully satisfy penis-envy, the child must be male (which would condemn over half of all women to inevitable neurosis):

She hopes for a son; he would be strong and dark; she would call him George; and this idea of having a male child was like an expected revenge for all her impotence of the past. A man, at least, is free; he can explore all passions and all countries, overcome obstacles, taste of the most distant pleasures. But a woman is always hampered. Being inert as well as pliable, she has against her the weakness of the flesh and the inequity of the law. . . .

She gave birth on a Sunday at about six o'clock, as the sun was rising.

"It's a girl!" said Charles.

She turned her head away and fainted.

Unable to obtain a phallus by "phallic proxy" (Luce Irigaray, *Speculum of the Other Woman*), Emma seeks to satisfy her desire to change sex through transvestism. Partial at the beginning of the novel, the disguise is completed just before Emma's death:

Like a man, she wore a tortoise-shell eyeglass thrust between two buttons of her blouse.

She parted [her hair] on one side and rolled it under, like a man's.

"[How could] I go riding without proper clothes?"

"You must order a riding outfit," he answered.

The riding habit ["amazone"] decided her.

On that day of Mid-Lent she did not return to Yonville; that evening she went to a masked ball. She wore velvet breeches, red stockings, a peruke, and a three-cornered hat cocked over one ear.

But, as Sartre demonstrates, for Flaubert sexuality belongs to the realm of the imagination; disguise is, then, only an *analogon* of Emma's imaginary sex. In the last analysis, it is only on the imaginary plane, i.e., on the plane of the role *played* in the couple, that Emma's growing virility asserts itself. The order of her affairs, Rodolphe before Léon, thus assumes its meaning: whereas in her relationship with Rodolphe Emma plays the female role, traditionally passive, in her relationship with Léon the roles are reversed: "he was becoming her mistress rather than she his."

It is not by chance that the writing apprenticeship and the "virility apprenticeship," if I may call it that, follow paths which ultimately converge at the time of Emma's affair with Léon, for their affair marks the triumph of the imaginary over the real, this being the precondition of all writing. If, insofar as the effect *on* the real is concerned, Homais's writing surpasses Emma's, considered in terms of the "reality effect," it is without any doubt Emma's (Flaubert's) writing that surpasses Homais's, for the "reality effect" can only be achieved through a total renunciation of any real satisfaction, can only be the just reward of sublimation, i.e., castration. For Flaubert writing thus has a sex, the sex of an assumed lack, the feminine sex.

It would seem, however, that all these oppositions are outweighed by Flaubert's radical distrust of language in general, a distrust evident in Emma's most bitter discovery, namely that "everything was a lie." For the Flaubert of *Madame Bovary* language is constantly undermined by its potential for lying, lying in the largest sense of the term, including hyperbole as well as the willful distortion of facts, and mystified idealization as well as cynical reductionism. The generalization of lying erases both the differences between forms of writing and the differences between writing and speech. Emma's letters and Homais's published pieces thus participate in the same "a-mimesis": both he and she depart from reality, embellishing facts, adjusting them to their needs. They "invent"—"Then Homais invented incidents." On the other hand, Emma's idealization—"irrealization," Sartre would say—of Léon on paper is only the resumption, the materialization of the oral self-idealization of the two lovers that occurs on the occasion of their reunion in Rouen:

> This was how they would have wished it to be, *each setting up an ideal* to which they were now trying to adapt their past life. Besides, *speech is like a rolling machine that always stretches the sentiment it expresses.* (my italics)

Things would be too simple if there were not at least one exception to the rule; hence old Rouault appears to escape the treason of language. His annual letter enjoys a harmony both metaphoric (letter = writer) and metonymic (letter = reality contiguous to the writer). The hiatus between writer, words, and things is here reduced to a minimum. In fact, in the Flaubertian system the opposite of lying is not telling the truth, but immediacy, because the least distance between the sender and the receiver, the writing subject and the Other, as well as that between man and Things, opens a gap through which lies penetrate:

> She held the coarse paper in her fingers for some minutes. A continuous stream of spelling mistakes ran through the letter, and Emma followed the kindly thought that crackled right through it like a hen half hidden in a hedge of thorns. The writing had been dried with ashes from the earth, for a little grey powder slipped from the letter on her dress, and she almost thought she saw her father bending over the hearth to take up the tongs.

Examined more closely, this model of paternal writing is in fact threatened from all sides. In spite of the spelling mistakes and the "intradiagetic" metaphor which guarantee the writer's adherence to words and things, the gap is there, manifest in the form of a lack: thought is compared to a "half hidden" hen. Adherence is thus only partial, and if this letter conveys writing-matter (letter + ashes), it is the matter itself that represents "the price to be paid": the symbolic Father is the dead Father.

Two consequences follow from this. First, for the characters who, unlike old Roualt, maintain relations with the world that are strongly mediated by written as well as spoken language, such as Emma, there is only one way in which to enjoy immediacy, and that is to step outside language. The two great erotic scenes of the novel link bliss (*jouissance*), plenitude, with the suspension of all linguistic communication. The initiation by Rodolphe culminates in one of the great Flaubertian silences, to borrow another expression from Genette:

> Silence was everywhere. . . . Then far away, beyond the wood, on the other hills, she heard a vague, prolonged cry, a voice which lingered, and in silence she heard it mingling like music with the last pulsations of her throbbing nerves.

If in this sense the spoken word is supplanted by a nonarticulated, a-semantic cry, in the coach scene the written word is torn to shreds, reduced to insignificance:

> One time, around noon, in the open country, . . . a bare hand appeared under the yellow canvas curtain, and threw out *some scraps of paper that scattered* in the wind, alighting further off like white butterflies on a field of red clover all in bloom. (my italics)

The euphoric form of the letter is thus the sperm-letter: in *Madame Bovary,* as in *The Temptation of Saint Anthony,* happiness is "being matter."

But if fictional characters, these "paper beings," find their happiness beyond or without language, what of the writer who is condemned to work in an articulate and signifying language? The writer cannot be for Flaubert but a pursuer of lies, making do for want of something better, with available means, i.e., language, language which is always both judge and plaintiff, source of lies and condemner of lies, poison and antidote, *pharmakon.* There is in *Madame Bovary* a character who appears to fulfill this prophylactic function. It is, as if by chance, a doctor, Doctor Larivière, a character with quasi-divine attributes: "The apparition of a god would not have caused more commotion." Note in what terms Flaubert describes his diagnostic gifts:

> His glance, more penetrating than his scalpels, looked straight into your soul, and would *detect any lie,* regardless how well hidden. (my italics)

These are exactly the same terms that Flaubert uses to define his stylistic ideal when, in a letter to Louise Colet contemporary with the writing of *Madame Bovary,* he criticizes Lamartine for not having "this medical view of life, this view of Truth." Truth, it must be remembered, is for Flaubert a matter of style. To be true, the writer need only substitute for the doctor's look the equivalent instrument in his art, i.e., his style:

> A style . . . precise like scientific language . . . a style that would penetrate into ideas like the probe of a stylet.

The structural homology of the two sentences in question, with, on the one hand, the scalpel-glance which "looked straight into your soul," and on the other the "stylet-style" which "penetrates into ideas," underscores the identity of scriptural approach and surgical procedure. There is nothing less passive, less feminine, than the relationship with language known as "les affres du style" (pains of style): the reader of the correspondence concerning *Madame Bovary* cannot be impressed with the aggressive and even sadistic relationship of Flaubert with the sentences and paragraphs of his novel that he sets about dissecting, unscrewing, undoing, unwriting, to use expressions found throughout his letters. To convey the inarticulate, one must disarticulate. As Sartre observes, "style is the silence of discourse, the silence in discourse, the imaginary and secret end of the written word" (*The Family Idiot*).

Flaubert's stylistic ideal completes his writing ideal; if Flaubert's writing refers to what one might call, playing a bit on Kristeva's terms, a "gyno-text," then his style aspires to a "phallo-text," a masculine "pheno-text":

> I love above all else nervous, substantial, clear sentences with flexed muscles and a rugged complexion: I like male, not female, sentences.
>
> (*Extrait de la correspondance*)

In the last analysis the "bizarre androgyn" is neither Flaubert (Sartre) nor Emma (Baudelaire), but the book, locus of the confrontation, as well as the interpenetration of *animus* and *anima,* of the masculine and the feminine.

By definition a *restricted* thematic study cannot claim to be all-encompassing. We are thus able to take note of a final demarcation separating the new thematic criticism from the old: concerned with thematic structure or, better still, structuring themes, new criticism must not go beyond the framework of the individual novel (poem, drama). (This does not, of course, exclude intertextual allusions and references.) Defining the corpus in this manner, restricted thematics reintroduces a diachronic dimension into the always synchronic or a-chronic apprehension of traditional thematic criticism, thereby substituting "a new hermeneutic, one that is syntagmatic, or metonymic" for "the classical hermeneutic that was paradigmatic (or metaphoric)" (Genette, "Table ronde" in *Cahiers Marcel Proust*). As we have observed, the writer/speech paradigm overdetermines not only the actantial distribution of characters but also the consecutive progression of the narrative sequences. I mean *overdetermine* because a thematic approach cannot by itself account for the multiple functioning of a text, but, given its "intent," one cannot really do without it.

The Biographer as Literary Critic: Sartre's Flaubert and *Madame Bovary*

Hazel Barnes

In his notes for the fourth volume [of *The Family Idiot*], which would have concentrated on *Madame Bovary,* Sartre asks, "Why write the first three volumes if one does not find them again on each page of the fourth?" It would be inconceivable for him to have meant by this that the enhancement of our understanding of *Madame Bovary* as a literary work was the sole justification of all that preceded. Obviously, he felt that if his method had been accurately applied, a discussion of the book would inevitably bring us back constantly to points established earlier. It is probably in much the same spirit that he has remarked that "anyone could write the fourth volume" by simply drawing the logical conclusions from the interpretation already laid down and continuing to apply the same hermeneutic. I suspect this statement lies somewhere between false modesty and sheer rhetoric. All the same, I think Sartre perhaps does feel that the three volumes of *The Family Idiot* can be taken as constituting a unified and not obviously truncated study in a way that would have been impossible if he had been forced to stop after the first or second volume. The study of *Madame Bovary* was to have shown how the work was a totalization of Flaubert as a "singular universal" expressing his period uniquely. If Sartre's interpretation proved to be convincing, it would not only add to our understanding of the novel and its author, but would offer the test and proof, so to speak, of Sartre's method. I suspect that for devotees of literature the fourth volume might have been the most interesting of all, and some

From *Sartre and Flaubert.* © 1981 by the University of Chicago. University of Chicago Press, 1981.

readers would doubtless have been content to enjoy the harvest without following Sartre's laborious tilling of the soil. Yet I find myself wondering if he would actually have written the final volume even if his health had not failed him. While seemingly knowing no limit in his exhaustive exploration of current projects, he never felt inclined to return for further amplification and clarification to ground already explored. The truth is that in the three existing volumes we have considerable information as to how Sartre would interpret *Madame Bovary,* both the work itself and its connection with the life of the author. His notes for the concluding volume offer certain new formulations and much elaboration, but nothing that suggests a startlingly different approach which could not have been anticipated. In this sense only I think, not that "anybody could write the fourth volume," but that any reader of the first three would know how to read *Madame Bovary* from a Sartrean perspective.

It would be idiotic to attempt to construct what the unwritten work might have been—in the manner that classical scholars try to reconstruct lost Greek tragedies on the basis of ancient plot summaries, vase paintings, etc. What does seem to me to be worth doing is to examine what Sartre has actually said about the novel, both in scattered passages in the published work and in the unpublished notes. And first I should say something about the notes. They are precisely that—*notes.* They are in no way an outline of a projected work. There are no completed sections, rarely even a fully worked-out paragraph. They are the first preliminary notations by an author getting ready to write a book which has not yet fully taken shape. They are distressingly like one's own efforts in the early, still disorganized stage of writing. The notes include comments on or by other critics and biographers of Flaubert, references to relevant passages in Flaubert's *Correspondence,* some detailed analysis of tense progressions in passages from *Madame Bovary,* a few somewhat random observations about style, descriptions, symbols, dialogue, etc. In addition and most important are interpretive observations of key points to be made concerning the characters or basic theme of the novel, repeated (sometimes in the same words) throughout the unorganized pages. Obviously, any use of these notes requires the greatest caution. It would be entirely unfair to deal with these private jottings as one would with a printed passage from a completed work. Yet when important points are made clearly, more than once, and particularly when they are closely related to ideas already expressed earlier in *The Family Idiot,* it seems fair to make use of this material in an effort to understand as fully as possible Sartre's reading of Flaubert's most admired book.

We may consider Sartre's contributions from [two of] the three points of view that have interested him: . . . the autobiographical reflections, [and the] formal aspects of style and structure.

Autobiographical Reflections

The significant connections between *Madame Bovary* and its author fall into two groups: those that seem to throw light on Flaubert's relations with other members of the family, and those that show him projecting aspects of himself in his characters, not only in Emma but also in Léon and, if Sartre is correct, even in Charles.

Looking first at reflections of his family relationships, we come immediately to the problem of Dr. Achille-Cléophas Flaubert. Obviously, Charles is not to be taken as a portrait of Gustave's father (or brother either), but Sartre thinks that Flaubert was not above taking a certain pleasure in making the dim-witted Charles a representative of the medical profession, even if he never qualified as a full-fledged physician. There is at least one parallel between Charles and the director of the hospital at Rouen: it appears that Achille-Cléophas, too, once attempted unsuccessfully to operate on a clubfoot. The portrait of Dr. Larivière, who is called in for consultation when Emma is dying, is almost certainly based on Gustave's father, and most critics have taken it to be a flattering one, a tribute offered by filial piety. Sartre finds this incredibly naive. Who is right? On the surface, at least, the description seems wholly admiring. We are told that the doctor was one of the old-time philosophical physicians, who disdained honors, who were fanatically devoted to the art of medicine, which they practiced "with enthusiasm and wisdom." His students so revered him that they imitated him down to the details of his clothing. But even in this laudatory paragraph, there is a suspicious hint of self-complacent arrogance.

> And so he went his way, full of that *majesté débonnaire* which is given by the consciousness of a great talent, of fortune, and forty years of a hard-working, irreproachable existence.

Almost everything here is potentially two-edged. *Débonnaire* can mean "meek" (it is so used to translate the key phrase in the third Beatitude), but frequently it is closer to the idea of "goodnatured" or "easygoing." With the word *majesté* it conveys the idea of "condescending." *Fortune,* in French as in English, may refer to either luck or personal wealth. Flaubert's choice of words is a bit dubious if he intended an unalloyed compliment. Sartre argues that if Flaubert had wanted to pay tribute to his father, it would have been more natural to introduce the doctor in a situation where he could effect a cure. As it is, the great doctor is brought into a situation where he is helpless to do anything. Then there is the statement that after talking with Charles, Dr. Larivière left with Dr. Canivet, "who didn't care either" (i.e., who also did not want) to see Emma die under his hands. But Sartre omits to mention that Dr. Larivière, witnessing Charles's distress, could not hold back a tear, which fell on his shirtfront.

Is Flaubert making little digs which perhaps he would not acknowledge even to himself? I suggest that our answer depends on how we respond to the account of the doctor's dinner with Homais. Dr. Larivière certainly sums up the druggist when he reassures Mme Homais's anxiety for her husband's health by saying, "It is not his blood that is thick." Are we to think that at this meeting we have the true scientist contrasted with the pseudoscientist who makes a travesty of all science? Or is Flaubert saying that both represent that shallow rationalism which can neither understand nor help those whose souls cry out for something more than science? We may note that there is no suggestion that Dr. Larivière's sympathy for Charles and Emma in any way prevented his thorough enjoyment of the delicacies Homais ordered for their dinner.

Baudelaire, in his review of *Madame Bovary*, recognized both that Flaubert had incarnated himself in his heroine and that in so doing he bestowed upon her certain masculine traits. Insofar as possible he "stripped himself of his own sex and made himself a woman." In her energy and ambitions, and even as "dreamer," "Madame Bovary remained a man. Like Pallas in armor sprung from the brain of Zeus, this bizarre androgynous being retained all the seductions of a virile soul in a charming feminine body." In *Search for a Method* Sartre indicated that in a study of Flaubert, it would be important to make a phenomenological study of Emma Bovary in order to understand the meaning of Flaubert's metamorphosis of himself into a woman.

> [We must ask,] what the artistic transformation of male into female means in the nineteenth century (we must study the context of *Mlle de Maupin,* etc.), and finally, just who Gustave Flaubert *must have been* in order to have within the field of his possibles the possibility of portraying himself as a woman. The reply is independent of all biography, since this problem could be posed in Kantian terms: "Under what conditions is the feminization of experience possible?"

While Sartre has not been able to carry through with all of his ambitious program, the published volumes include considerable discussion of Flaubert's "femininity" and its presence in *Madame Bovary,* and Sartre has given a few hints at least on how all this would be related to the social milieu.

We have already considered [elsewhere] Sartre's view of Flaubert's sexuality as connected with his constitutional passivity, his desire for the "phallic mother," and the accompanying nostalgia for androgyny, expressed both in the wish-fantasy of his romantic hero (in *November*) that he might have the experience of being a woman and in Flaubert's equally unrealistic wish that Louise Colet might be at once woman and man. The most obvious reflections of all this in the novel are to be found in the episodes with Emma and Léon. In Sartre's discussion of these what emerges most strikingly is the fact that to some degree Flaubert has alternately—sometimes perhaps even simultaneously—identified himself with both Emma and Léon. Baudelaire claimed that Emma was masculine in her sensuality and her pursuit of pleasure. Possibly from the nineteenth-century male's point of view this was so. Sartre, as we have seen [elsewhere], takes the same attitude, viewing the entire relation of Emma to Leon as based on a "perversion" of their natural sex roles. (When he speaks of "perversion" he is not making a moral judgment. He defines the term as "taking to the limit an erotic image which is based on the imaginary.") Speaking for myself, I find all of this comment on Emma's "masculinity" a bit exaggerated. That she would have had a wistful yearning for the more free and adventurous life that she imagined to be open to a man is only natural for any woman in a society which opens more doors for men than for women. This is especially true for Emma, who always believed that an alteration in her situation—whether another man or a different city—would perhaps allow her to realize her dreams. Flaubert explicitly says this in the course of describing Emma's pregnancy.

> She wished for a son; he would be strong and dark, and she would call him George; and this idea of having a male as her child was like a hoped-for revenge for all her past impotences. A man, at least, is free; he can explore passions and countries, overcome obstacles, taste the most distant pleasures. But a woman is continually held back.

When she learns that she has borne a girl, Emma faints. Decades before Freud, Flaubert writes of a woman who, frustrated in her own desires, hopes to compensate by vicariously living the life of her son. The motivation he supplies is a cultural one, not the famous "penis envy" hypothe-sized by Freud. The passage shows also a sensitivity on Flaubert's part to circumstances not resembling his own which Sartre is reluctant to recog-nize and which, it must be admitted, is seldom present in Flaubert's atti-tude toward women outside of fiction.

There is nothing masculine in Emma's relations with Rodolphe. The only suggestion of an exchange of sex roles with Charles is the description of the pair on the first morning after the wedding night, and this quite clearly refers solely to their respective reactions to their first sexual union. If Charles, rather than Emma, resembles the newly awakened deflowered virgin, this is because the experience meant more to him than it did to her. Like the wedding guests, we may wonder why but cannot know. Inas-much as Charles certainly had full sexual relations with his first wife, I think the text, as concerns him, refers to enhanced emotional experience or what we might call erotic rather than sexual in the narrow sense. Sartre refers to a notation in Flaubert's plans for the novel, which says that Emma received no pleasure from her husband. We may easily believe that the experience was disappointing to her whether there was technically a physical satisfaction or not. The point is not important for our concern here. Nothing on that morning after suggests that she was the aggressive partner. With the weak and relatively inexperienced Léon, Emma, the pu-pil of Rodolphe, naturally dominates, but this is hardly to say that she does not remain fully feminine unless one is to cling to an outmoded view of what feminine sexuality is. I agree, however, that what Flaubert has told us of the quality of Emma's and Léon's amorous relations is impor-tant, and it is legitimate to ask whether we may find here reflections of Flaubert himself.

Insofar as the identification with Emma is concerned, Sartre does not emphasize the explicitly sexual. To the degree that he was fascinated by the idea of living in imagination the life of any of his characters, Flaubert may have derived a particular satisfaction from imagining as fully as possi-ble what it would be like to be a woman. The conventional equation of femininity and passivity may have held a special appeal for him. Beyond what Sartre has pointed out apropos of Emma's union with Rodolphe in the forest, we might find a special significance in the fact that the pantheis-tic aspect is inextricably linked with a feminine sexual fulfillment. Once again, I think passivity is the essential thing here. But it is possible that in Flaubert's mind passive receptivity to these visionary moments and his imaginary femininity were closely associated. On the whole, however, it is his deepest aspirations toward beauty, the eternal, and the more than humanly real that he both incarnates and to some degree ridicules in Emma. To put this self in a woman may reflect a feeling on Flaubert's part that this aspect of his character was more feminine than truly virile. We recall his complaint that women possessed a large degree of the artist's innate special sensitivity, but that they almost inevitably betray it by linking it with the particular erotic. This is Emma's error. I cannot go so far as to agree with Sartre when he says in the notes that "the subjectivity of Emma is not that of a man but of a man who believes himself a woman." He adds that a woman would have portrayed Emma differently. True, and so would a different man. I agree that if Flaubert's own psychological traits had been different, he would not have been able to give us Emma. But that Emma as a character is "a disguised man" I cannot accept. The question of how much in her is also Flaubert is a quite different thing.

Sartre lays more stress on the degree to which Flaubert has identified his own sexual inclinations with Léon's. He does not mean, of course, that Flaubert has modeled Léon as a person after himself. Sartre observes that Flaubert disliked Léon, partly perhaps because he resembled Ernest Chevalier, who also posed as a romantic in his youth but later became a typical bourgeois. But Léon in bed with Emma offers some interesting parallels to what we know of Flaubert. Léon is indeed a male who plays a role closer to that conventionally assigned to women.

To Léon Emma was the Angel and the Mistress. At times he felt uneasily that he was the one possessed by her, but this half-resentful attitude belonged to reflective moments away from her. In her presence he experienced the same kind of self-effacement, the fulfilling loss of self that Emma felt with Rodolphe.

> Often in looking at her, it seemed to him that his soul, escaping toward her, spread out like a wave above the outline of her head and descended, drawn down into the whiteness of her breast.

What is different here is the sense of being absorbed into the other or blended with her, and—though Sartre does not comment on it—there is something faintly reminiscent of the symbiotic relation of mother and infant.

At other times Flaubert describes something almost frenetic in their relations, especially on Emma's part, and Léon is put off.

> There was on that brow, covered with cold drops, on those trembling lips, in those distraught eyes something extreme,

vague and mournful, which seemed to Léon to slip subtly between them as if to separate them.

Sartre finds in these descriptions echoes of both Flaubert's imagined sexual
fantasies and his actual relation with Louise. In Emma, Léon has found the
dream mistress of the hero of *November,* the woman adored and feared,
who ruins men with her whims, who devours her lover with kisses that
suck out his very soul. There is a still an older echo. Flaubert shows
Emma liking to play the role of mother. Sartre claims that Léon fulfills,
so far as is consistent with Flaubert's surface realism, the dream of the
phallic mother. He is like the dependent male child, roused to virility, so
as to penetrate and possess the caressing mother.

Sartre sees one very specific connection between art and life in the cab
episode, and he believes that it helps to explain Flaubert's mockery of the
lovers. The Goncourt brothers recorded in their journal an occasion in
1862 when Flaubert told them about the beginning of his involvement
with Louise. He described how it all took shape in a ride in a cab, with
him playing the role of one disgusted with life, filled with Byronic gloom,
yearning for suicide. The game so much amused and disgusted him that
from time to time he stuck his nose out the door so as to give himself
relief in laughing. The Goncourts looked on all this quite unfavorably and
Sartre declares flatly that Flaubert's recital was the act of a cad. He and
Louise (even after the affair was over) moved in the same circles; he could
count on the two Goncourts to repeat the story, and the now well-known
cab scene in the novel would add to the hilarity. What Sartre thinks Flaubert was doing, both in his conversation and in the novel, was to give vent
to a rancorous memory. A carriage ride with Louise shortly before his first
night with her played an important part in their sentimental history. The
love-making was purely verbal or implied. Louise's child was present, and
there were probably no closed certains. But Sartre believes that the "line"
Flaubert describes to the Goncourts was in all probability his timid attempt
to reveal to Louise something of himself, either as he was or as he had
been in the past. It may have been partly role-playing, but at least the role
was one that Gustave had played for himself for some years. In a letter to
Louise which Sartre cites, he speaks of having "begun by showing her his
wounds." At twenty-five, Flaubert, though he had considerable experience with prostitutes and a glamorous courtesan in Egypt, was unsure of
himself with a woman of Louise's social standing. Sartre notes that Flaubert was inadequate their first night together though he easily made up for
it on subsequent occasions. Sartre claims that the memory of his lack of

assurance rankled and that it was this that led him to introduce an altered version of the ride in *Madame Bovary*. In the cab in Paris there may have been some question as to who was seducing whom. At Rouen, Léon is the aggressor, Emma the dupe. But both are the objects of the scornful laugh of the giant who looks down from above on all this sorry foolishness of the human species. The laugh is also that of the Garçon and the jeering schoolboys at the lycée.

In the *Critique* Sartre indicated that if we are to understand the meaning of a male author's imaginative metamorphosis of himself into a woman, we must learn what this would mean in the context of his particular society, one which had produced, among other things, Gautier's *Mademoiselle de Maupin*. In his discussion of the Knights of Nothingness, he gave part of the answer: the artist's feeling that aesthetic sensitivity required a certain feminization, linked with the idea that success as an artist must be paid for by failure as a man. The mention of *Mademoiselle de Maupin* suggests to me something else. The novel concerns a young woman who enjoys sexual relations with both another woman and a man, who have been lovers of each other. The suggestion is that each of the pair could experience complete love only with a person who combined the essential qualities of both male and female beauty and personality. Their relation with each other, we are led to believe, will be enriched by their mutual adoration of the androgynous ideal. Mlle de Maupin herself, of course, enjoys the fulfillment of both sexes, albeit in perverted form (I use the adjective in the Sartrean sense). At the end of the book the heroine leaves both her lovers after a single night and goes on, in the same disguise, to pursue more adventures. She is the all but literal fulfillment of the fantasy of the hero of *November* and, if Sartre is right, of Flaubert. More than this, she satisfies, insofar as is possible, the desire for an impossible totality of experience. We should be careful, however, not to confuse this androgyny with that sometimes proposed today as an ideal. There is no reformist tendency, no intent to question prevailing attitudes as to what properly constitutes male and female or to suggest that they be merged in a new concept of the person. Mademoiselle de Maupin first takes up her disguise in an effort to know what men really are apart from the roles they play in women's presence and to see if one of them might be worthy of her as person. She continues her disguise because she learns that no man respects women or can be trusted in his relations with them, and she admits that most women are what men believe them to be. At best, she stands for an unreal, purely romantic escape from the limits of our real human condition. She is a male artist's projection of himself in a female body, and she is closer to Plato's double-sexed creature in the *Symposium* than to a real man *or* woman in the nineteenth century or in our own.

Sartre has noted a number of autobiographical details in *Madame Bovary,* many of which have been mentioned by other biographers and do not seem to me of great significance either for our understanding of Flaubert or of Sartre's own intentions. There are two groups of observations which are original and more important; the first of these concerns Emma, the second refers to Charles.

Any reader of *Madame Bovary* must be aware of the consistent pattern in Emma's responses to her great disappointments. On each occasion there is a repetition and an intensification. After the ball at Vaubyessard, which both illumined her life and poisoned it by seeming to reveal a real world in which romantic dreams might be satisfied but one closed to her, she falls into a psychosomatic decline, a mental torpor with real physical symptoms of ill health. After Léon leaves for Paris, the same thing happens; Flaubert himself points up the parallel: "The bad days of Tostes began again." When Rodolphe leaves her, Emma nearly dies of "brain fever." At the end, she commits suicide. Critics have pointed out that just before she goes to get the poison, she experiences a sense of disorientation, with hallucinations of fiery balls exploding in the air, which seems to recall Flaubert's seizure at Pont-l'Évêque. Sartre recognizes all this, remarking on the psychosomatic implications, with obvious reference to Flaubert's own life. He comments particularly on Emma's illness after Rodolphe's departure and links it with Flaubert in two ways. Emma reads Rodolphe's parting letter alone in the attic. Looking out the window, she is tempted to kill herself. The abyss before her, the glancing light and blue heavens, the ground of the square below that appears to be moving, the floor that seems to dip "like a tossing boat," all impel her to let herself go. She is stopped by the sound of Charles's voice calling her. Sartre thinks that this near suicide is a recollection of a similar experience of Flaubert's. We know he had thought of suicide during those early years in Paris; Jules comes close to throwing himself off a bridge. Sartre relates the passage to one in *November,* which, like this, merges the idea of death with overtones of the childhood sense of being lost, or dissolved in nature. The young man lies down near the sea and is tempted to let the waves wash over him. "The voices of the abyss were calling him; the waves were opening like a tomb ready then to close over him and to wrap him in their liquid folds." Both the "abyss" and the "sea" have been retained in Emma's near delirium even though she stands in an attic overlooking the village square. Sartre calls to our attention, too, the significance of Emma's being at a height from which she would throw herself down—Flaubert's old theme of verticality and fall.

Sartre finds an echo of Flaubert's own fall in Emma's subsequent illness. Flaubert tells us that she developed "brain fever," a nineteenth-century designation for any illness which involved loss or distortion of consciousness, particularly when it followed after some kind of psychic shock. What happened first with Emma was that she cried out and fell prostrate, rigid on the floor. Obviously the description evokes the memory of Flaubert's fall in the carriage. Sartre brings the parallel still closer and uses it as evidence that Flaubert was fully aware of the response of his own body to his psychological dilemma and recognized that his seizure and illness were a response and an adaptation. Sartre writes,

> The proof of this is that his Madame Bovary later on will make explicitly a somatization-response. Abandoned by Rodolphe, she falls ill, a terrible bout of fever seems to put her life in danger; and then, at the end of some weeks, she finds herself cured of fever and of love, both at once. Or, if you prefer, love *is made into a fever* in order that it may be liquidated by means of psychic disorders.

Sartre points to one other, less dramatic resemblance between Gustave and his heroine: their love of luxury. Flaubert is quite explicit in showing how Emma's dreams of love were inextricably bound up with longings for luxurious surroundings. In a sense, the ball at Vaubyessard awakened her to the possibility of the real existence of both love and luxury and intensified their interdependence. Flaubert himself did not live in luxury, but Sartre argues that he envied those who did. We have observed how the word "mistress" conjured up for him associated ideas of passion and wealthy splendor. He longed to have the superfluous in order that he might be freed from the power of need. Sartre claims that in his nostalgic regrets at the collapse of France in 1870 there was a barely concealed longing for its past luxuriance. "Even every material elegance is finished for a long time."

With respect to Flaubert's self-identification with Charles, we must be very careful. Obviously Sartre does not intend to take this very far. In the opening pages of the novel, "Charbovary" is clearly contrasted with the "we" of the rest of the class. In passages that Flaubert decided not to include, the separation is stressed still more. In fact, it was by a negative portrait of Charles that Flaubert described himself and the others. "How little he resembled all the rest of us!" Charles did not read late at night, long for Paris, and strike Byronic poses. Still Sartre believes that the picture of Charles's isolation as the sorry butt of the other pupils may represent in exaggerated form Gustave's recollections of himself in the early days when he felt himself to be misunderstood and ridiculed. Even the mumbled "Charbovary" may reflect the young Gustave's feelings of frustration apropos of language. This view, of course, fits in with Sartre's feeling that Flaubert wants us to "weep for Charles"—with more sincerity, I suggest, than was in Dr. Larivière's solitary tear. I think one cannot go very far with the Flaubert-as-Charles notion. And indeed Sartre, too, notes the several times that Flaubert describes Charles's love in terms suggesting nutrient—making love regularly as one takes dessert after dinner, enjoying his remembered joy as one has the aftertaste of truffles, hardly images to apply to a sensitive hero. But it well may be that Flaubert retained a certain sympathy with a man who felt deeply without trying to express himself in words and who was therefore credited with no depth of feeling.

For Sartre, however, the autobiographical significance of *Madame Bovary* is found not only in incidental reflections of episodes or in Flaubert's attributing to one of the characters particular attitudes of his own, whether sexual or intellectual. What is essential is that his overall intention in the book and the life project of Flaubert himself are—if not identical—closely harmonious. This will become more evident if we look at Satre's plans for analyzing the form and style of the novel.

Style and Structure

While I would never say that Sartre's interpretation of *Madame Bovary* is due to the influence of Baudelaire, it is amazing how much of what he has said could be viewed as an elaboration of points made in the poet's famous review of the novel. We have already remarked on Flaubert's projection of himself in his heroine, Emma's "masculinity," and the similarity of theme in *Madame Bovary* and *The Temptation of Saint Anthony*. There is another passage which may serve as an introduction to our present discussion; this one, however, will show us Baudelaire's limitations as a critic as well as his gifted insight. He imagines Flaubert as having said to himself:

> I do not need to concern myself with style, with picturesque ordering, with the description of places; I possess all these qualities to a superabundant degree; I shall proceed relying on analysis and logic, and I shall prove that all subjects are indifferently

good or bad according to the way they are treated and that the most commonplace can become the best.

Baudelaire recognized that the true subject of the novel was something more than the chronicle of the affairs of a "provincial adulteress"; what he failed to see was that Flaubert effected his transformation, not by analysis and logic, but precisely by his deliberate, highly conscious, and careful concern with style—in descriptions and in his ordering of every paragraph and sentence. It is style that allows him, as Sartre puts it, to seem to be treating one reality while actually writing of another.

"*Madame Bovary* is a metaphor for *The Temptation of Saint Anthony.*" This mingling of the realistic concrete with the metaphysical both gives the novel its value and, Sartre admits, results in the "falsity" of its style. In moving from the trials of the saint to the story of the "provincial adulteress" and her unfortunate husband, it is as though Flaubert said to himself—or perhaps, as Sartre suggests, someone else said to him—"Instead of imagining the imaginary, imagine the real." For Flaubert, "to imagine the real" would be to *derealize* an actual event (whether specific or typical) by giving it a meaning which it did not have for those who lived it, to make it serve as a vehicle to convey a more universal truth perceived by the author. Above all, it would be to tell a story in which the most important things were those that were not said, in which *l'indisable* would be communicated. All of this must be done with no distortion of everyday reality in the details of the narrative and without moral commentary by the author, who must remain impersonal. It can be accomplished only by *style,* which Sartre himself has defined as a way of saying three or four things at once, of providing in a single sentence a plurality of meanings, some of which may be contradictory. In the hands of a Flaubert, style may lead us to hold two points of view at once without fully realizing that we are doing so.

Flaubert once expressed the wish that he might write a "book about nothing." This disdain for subject matter and specific content reflects his wish to substitute imagination entirely for reality and to keep art free of material restrictions. We have observed his feeling that words betrayed poetic vision and genuine emotion. Sartre claims that Flaubert's style originates precisely in this resentment against words.

In the notes Sartre makes some general statements about how Flaubert conveys his sense of two realities, and he provides numerous examples of detailed analysis of stylistic points. Flaubert liked to think of himself as a "writer" rather than as a "novelist." Sartre suggests that perhaps one rea-

son for this was reluctance to consider himself a mere "teller of tales."
"The novel will be the mirror of the world." It must tell a story, but "this
story must be at the same time a totalization of the world. This is the case
with Madame Bovary. The world reveals its nothingness in her and in her
death." The author "will show that every life which elects to live is a Fall
and suffering [*mal*], by two examples: Emma and the realist Charles who
has no imagination but who is devoured by the imagination of a dead
woman." *Madame Bovary* is a "novel of failure and of fatality. It presents
not causes but maturations." As a story the book unfolds a clear temporal
sequence; as a totalization it seems to deny the passage of time. "Since the
events about to be recorded here, nothing has changed at Yonville." The
tale seems to be told us long after the central characters are dead. The last
sentence, which informs us of the honor Homais has just received, is in
the present tense; this is the laugh that eternally mocks all higher aspirations. At one point Charles feels as if he were surrounded by evil influ-
ences. In the midst of her happiness with Rodolphe, Emma asks herself
why she should feel so sad. Death and emptiness are present everywhere.
Sometimes the narrative and style seem to be at odds with each other; ultimately they come together. One of Sartre's compressed notes sums it up
as follows:

> Thus the adventure of the Bovary couple is seen from two
> points of view: (1) Metaphysically: movement is annulled, rest
> remains. (2) Socially: they were unable to adapt. Two times:
> the immutable and the time of degradation.

Emma herself is not just a "provincial adulteress"; she is, Sartre says,
Saint Anthony, and she is "a myth." Like Flaubert, she is an "imaginary
person," but she lives in a world as real as the author could make it, the
"invented real." The world of the novel is not actually our world, but it
resembles ours. This is why, Sartre seems to tell us, the story of Emma
and Charles is offered to us as our own story—in metaphor.

Sartre has said that volume 4 would have been mostly a stylistic analysis. He has stated also that he intended to use certain "structuralist techniques," which he felt would be compatible with his own method if they
were properly applied. He added that for the most part he looks with dis-
approval on current literary research, which is overconcerned with formal-
ism and rhetoric. Both structuralists and linguists, in his opinion, treat
language too much as something external, divorced from human intentions. There is nothing in the notes that indicates just how Sartre held his
intended procedures to be related to structuralism. Most of what he does

seems to me not radically different from the approach used in prestructuralist criticism. Yet there is certain similarity between some of his analyses and the kind of linguistic investigation employed by a few recent Flaubert critics who have been influenced by structuralism. Even here, however, one will find Sartre relating particular uses of language to what he believes to be Flaubert's subjective intention rather than to the requirements of the text as a strictly objective, created work of art.

Sartre's specific observation on the structure and style of *Madame Bovary* may be grouped under three headings: the problem of narrative point of view; the author's attitude toward his characters, which includes both a consideration of irony and the problem of language as communication; descriptions of places and things.

The Narrator. Although Sartre gives no indication of having read Wayne Booth's *Rhetoric of Fiction,* he is clearly aware of the problem of what Booth calls "the authorial voice." The "omniscient author" may reflect the writer's ideas, but author and narrator are not the same. This, Sartre explains, is "because the author as person *invents* whereas the narrator tells *what happened.* . . . The author invents the capricious narrator who merely tells a story." As Booth has pointed out, the narrator, whether he intrudes with "dear reader" commentary or purports to be as impersonal as he is omniscient, is always a unique creation for the specific book in which he appears. He (or she, for the authorial voice need not be sexless simply because it is not individualized) sets the tone for the book and *is* the point of view as surely as if we were dealing with a fictional first-person narrator. Any narrator, Sartre says, is a mediator who stands between the book's "environment" and the reader. We may note that the narrator who most closely resembles the author still communicates to us only that aspect of his or her self which the author chooses to offer. In the case of someone like Flaubert, who has resolved "not to write himself in," the ideal of total impersonality is already betrayed in the choice of the narrator who is assigned the role of chronicler.

Of course the problem of the narrator in *Madame Bovary* is a complex one. Most of the time he seems to be the typical omniscient recorder of both outward events and internal reflection, the pure "authorial voice." But when we first meet him, he is presented as an eyewitness, one of "us" who were in the classroom on the day of Charles Bovary's first day at school. There is a suggestion of the relaxed tone of one who talks with us; indeed, Sartre claims that the novel as a whole shows traces of an oral style. What is the *real* identity of this man who first speaks to us? Sartre tells us that he is the second narrator of *November.* I think this insight is particularly apt. The dry tone, the irony (much further developed, of course, in *Madame Bovary*), the hidden sense that even in her romantic foolishness and falseness, his poor heroine is better than the people who surround her, and (most important of all) the way in which the narrator is sometimes outside as a mere acquaintance and then again privy to the most secret feelings of the character—all of these things are common to both narrators. If we accept Sartre's claim that the second narrator of *November* represents already the role that Flaubert had chosen for himself in contemplating his own life and past, then we may conclude that the resemblance is neither coincidental nor insignificant. Possibly it explains why Flaubert continued to be fond of this work of his adolescence and to allow some of his friends in later life to read it.

This is not to overlook the fact that there is considerable shift in narrative point of view beyond the initial movement from "we" to omniscient author. Sartre notes that we have two forms of the present witness even in the opening pages. At first the narrator seems to be one of the boys in the class at Rouen who sees Charles as a new student and stranger. Then suddenly we are given a quick survey of his family background and childhood, something which might just possibly have been provided by a member of the class who later became more closely acquainted with the Bovary family. Then come the words, "It would be impossible for any of us now to recall anything about him." After which, as Sartre points out, the narrator proceeds to tell us very intimate things about Charles, whom he knows very well. It is as though an impersonal "we" (what in English we call the "editorial we") had emerged out of the personal "we" of the schoolroom. But the chatty citizen of Rouen returns from time to time. He is implied in the sentence "Nothing has changed at Yonville," and is probably present in the last sentence of the book: "He has just received the cross of honor." Sartre points to other discontinuities. There is an unidentified "you" (*vous*) when we are told at the scene of the fair that "the housewives bumped into you with their big umbrellas, their baskets, and their babies." To whom does the "you" refer? "It is the readers, not as they sit reading the book but as if they had been present." Sartre cites another example of lack of precise placement: at the ball the viscount and Emma dance down to the end of a long gallery and disappear. "From whose point of view?" asks Sartre. Then there are the many modulations of tone. The book is "polyphonic," Sartre says, in that Emma's is not the only point of view that is important; we must see things through Charles's eyes as well and occasionally through those of Rodolphe or Léon or one of the other characters. But even when seeming to be inside the same character, the tone may change. We saw one example in the cab scene, but there are numerous less extreme examples where the narrator, who has been very close, will suddenly seem to hold his heroine at a distance, will move from reflecting her thoughts to commenting on them.

Sartre, like other critics, notes Flaubert's predilection for the indirect reporting of Emma's reactions (*le style indirect libre*). Rather than giving us internal monologue or stream of consciousness, he will tell us about her thoughts and feelings in such a way that one cannot quite be sure what is fact, what is Emma's own reflection, what is narrator's commentary. When Emma, the evening after being with Rodolphe, looks at her altered reflection in the mirror, the indirect style seems to give authenticity to her perception. In the statement, "She longed to die and to live in Paris," we obviously have the narrator's ironic summation of the contents of her reflections. And what of such a sentence as we find, for example, when Emma is desperately wondering to whom she might turn in order to prevent Charles from discovering that her financial recklessness has ruined him.

> The wish came to her to return to Lheureux: What good would it do? To write her father; it was too late; and perhaps now she began to repent of not having given in to the other [the notary].

In this particular instance the uncertainty of the "perhaps" may be the perfect description of Emma's state of mind. As applied to the narrator, it raises a question. Sartre points out that on many occasions the narrator will profess not to know the real reason for his character's reaction. He will tell us that Charles disapproves of Homais, possibly for one reason, possibly for another. Or he says that Emma herself does not know . . . "But if she doesn't know," asks Sartre, "is this any reason why the author should not know?" Or the omniscient narrator? Everything seems calculated to throw us off base, to prevent us from knowing exactly from what angle we are viewing what we read.

Sartre would explain this deliberate ambiguity and discontinuity as the result of Flaubert's insistence on maintaining the point of view of *le survol*. As author he assumes the stance of one who is viewing events from a vantage point outside time and space. Consequently he comprehends all points of view at once and will not allow his narrator to be restricted to one angle. Could he not have gained the same result by using simply the "omniscient author" without resorting to the "we" in the first chapter? Sartre does not take up this question directly. I would suggest that there might be two reasons for what Flaubert has done. First, we may note that the person who speaks to us out of the "we" is never individualized. He represents a collective point of view on how Charles looked to his peers— just as later we are told how Emma's conduct is regarded by the gossips in Yonville. Not formally but practically it is little more than an extended use of the indirect style applied to a group. As such it amounts to simply one more of the viewpoints that add up to constitute the all-embracing comprehension of the impersonal observer. It is important that *le survol* should include all points of view, not become simply one more of them. It cannot be allowed to seem to give unity and coherence to a reality that lacks them. Second, if we raise as a difficulty the argument that one cannot be simultaneously inside and out, Sartre might reply that this was something that Flaubert never recognized. The narrative point of view in *Madame Bovary* is the artistic development of Flaubert's form of revery when he simultaneously suffered and triumphed in the schoolroom at the lycée.

Jonathan Culler, in a study of Flaubert that acknowledges a heavy debt to Sartre and *The Family Idiot,* argues that already in his juvenile works, Flaubert recognized a basic dilemma: if he maintained a purely authorial stance, his *exempla* were obviously instances created to prove a point, hence carried no authority; a first-person confessional, on the other hand, could express only a biased judgment, therefore could not pronounce objective judgment on reality as a whole. In one sense, then, we may say that *Madame Bovary* is the solution. The author, by alternating between complicity and detachment, presents simultaneously a subjective, temporal experience and an impersonal nontemporal judgment on all human affairs. Culler goes a step farther. Just as he argues that the comment at the end of *November* is a mocking reminder that only in novels is it possible to "grasp this life as a meaningful whole," so we are not allowed to achieve a single, unifying point of view on events in *Madame Bovary.* The inconsistencies (as a realist would call them) are a deliberate means to force upon us the constant realization that we are reading a novel and that a real life cannot be read as a novel any more than Emma could realize her dreams as the literary heroines did. Shifts in narrative point of view force us to recall that we are reading a work of art just as, Culler argues, Flaubert's sentences are deliberately designed to call attention to themselves as language.

Are Culler's and Sartre's explanations mutually exclusive? In principle I do not think so. Sartre, too, recognizes that Flaubert wishes us to realize that unity, eternal meaning, and beauty belong in the realm of the unreal. But he is concerned with the question of *why* Flaubert is so insistent on the superiority of the imaginary. One particular passage in Sartre, however, has been sharply attacked by both Culler and Dominick LaCapra, who claim that Sartre's biographical interest in Flaubert has led him to make a false critical judgment. This is in the context of Sartre's interpretation of the cab episode. Culler writes, quoting from Sartre directly,

> Sartre judges the episode a failure because the shift in perspective "refers us to the malignant intention of the author. . . . It's the end of dramatic illusion: there are no longer characters, just puppets manipulated by a director." It is not a little ironic that Sartre, whose greatness derives from his overpowering theatrical sophistication, should condemn *Madame Bovary* in the name of dramatic illusion and the theory of the novel it implies. . . . The thematic projects which Sartre correctly identifies depend, in large measure, on the techniques of displacement and fragmentation which he finds disturbing. The reader would not be demoralized, after all, by a tale told from the point of view of an order which he could identify and adopt as his own.
>
> (*Flaubert: The Uses of Uncertainty*)

This last sentence is certainly true, and I think Sartre would agree. But I believe that Culler has misread Sartre's intention. Sartre does not condemn *Madame Bovary* nor even say that the passage in question is a failure in itself. Specifically, he claims that Flaubert has failed to achieve a particular end which he had set for himself. Sartre defines it in the form of a question:

> Has he succeeded, while remaining himself invisible, in sending an anonymous laugh, without laughers, to run from one page to the next, imposing itself on the readers without the author's emerging from his "impersonalism" and without having done anything but to deliver to them the itinerary of a particular cab during the afternoon of a particular day in a particular year?

Obviously he has not. Flaubert forces us to view the lovers' afternoon, not as they experience it or even as the reader might be inclined to see it, but as he himself wants to see it. But this is consistent with what he has done elsewhere in the novel. It is the juxtaposition of the author's immediate subjectivity and *le survol* that partially accounts for the sense of "two realities" and allows the shadow of one to fall upon the other. But *le survol* is always itself a fiction. If Sartre intended to leave the impression that Flaubert's personal malice had intruded so as to ruin the scene, Culler's criticism would be justified. But if he meant only that the presence of the giant and Gustave Flaubert is more apparent here than elsewhere and that we know the reason for it, I think Sartre is entirely right. I certainly cannot agree with LaCapra's statement: "The fiacre scene seems to be written from no one's point of view: it is almost 'pure' text, writing itself" (*A Preface to Sartre*). To accomplish this aim would have required the suppression of the coachman's comic bewilderment and indeed to make the description nothing but the itinerary of a coach on a certain day in a particular place, and it would hold no interest.

Attitude toward Characters. Sartre has expressed what I think is typical of readers' reactions to the characters in *Madame Bovary*.

> Reading Flaubert one is plunged into persons with whom one is in complete disaccord, who are irksome. Sometimes one feels with them, and then somehow they suddenly reject one's sympathy and one finds oneself again antagonistic to them.

Sartre explains this as the result of Flaubert's self-dislike. As his own creations and at times his self-projections, they are subject to the same sadomasochistic attitude he sustained in his personal relations with the world.

> He tortures them because they are himself, and also to show that other people and the world torture him. He also tortures them because they are not him and he is anyway vicious and sadistic and wants to torture others.
>
> ("Itinerary of a Thought")

Although the last sentence may be an overstatement, it does seem that Flaubert's characters (including the good Félicité) are punished by sufferings in inverse proportion to their merits. It is also true that Flaubert's irony, in *Madame Bovary* at least, prohibits any total empathy with any of the characters. Sartre has not elaborated on the manner in which the irony is sustained, perhaps because this subject has already been thoroughly discussed by critics. Culler points out that Flaubert preferred "verbal rather than situational irony." This is true, and I have noted that on the rare occasions when he does provide an ironic situation, he sometimes seems impelled to call our attention to it with an authorial comment, almost as though he could not let the situation speak for itself. For example, when Emma, just after refusing to sell herself to the notary, resolves to appeal to Rodolphe, Flaubert tells us in so many words, that "she was running to offer herself to that which had just now so outraged her, totally unaware of her prostitution." Usually the irony is much more subtle and is a function of the style itself, resulting from the deliberate use of words and sentences with a plurality of meanings. At times it is so delicate one can hardly be sure that it is there. A word or image will have the effect of slightly undermining the mood or tone of a passage, like the self-deprecating smile of one who puts himself forward. My own favorite example comes from the very passage that I quoted earlier to illustrate the nonverbal communication between Léon and Emma on the first evening at the hotel. The moment of silence is filled with an infinite sweetness, and the prevailing tone is one of tenderness. Yet it includes an image so strange as to be almost bizarre. "They sensed a humming in their heads as if something resonant had reciprocally escaped from the fixed pupils of their eyes." The mixture of auditory and visual, the overprecise localization of sensation and origin becomes ludicrous if one stops to analyze. Is this Flaubert's intention? I suspect so, and think that he also intended that it would be so without spoiling the dominant effect of the passage when read quickly. The ambivalence is characteristic of the entire novel.

In the notes Sartre makes several references to the lack of communication that generally exists between characters and that paradoxically is conveyed by means of their conversations. Direct speech is comparatively rare. When it occurs, Sartre says, we do not have true reciprocal dialogue, but rather "an alternation of monologues," at best "a simultaneity of discourse not understood rather than communication." Mostly it is at cross-purpose. Emma's abortive visit to the curé is one example, when the curé interprets her *"je souffre"* as referring to purely physical ailing and tells her to ask help of her husband. Emma and Charles outdo each other in offering to take on the burden of the trip to Rouen to consult Léon about the power of attorney. And so on. Most of what is said is insincere—Rodolphe's wooing at the fair, his impassioned protestation on their last night together, which owes its unusual intensity to his secret resolve to leave her. When a true message *is* conveyed, it is by means of a hidden conversation which has nothing to do with the actual words spoken; for example, Emma's first meeting with Léon. Sartre notes that there are a few occasions when the words are sincere, but then they are not taken as such—as when Rodolphe fails to believe in the depth of Emma's love for him because he has heard the same banal phrases from other lips obviously false. In the characters' relations with one another words destroy; only the rare nonverbal moment of communication unites. The author's words simultaneously describe a world which the overtones, the "silences between the words," undermine.

Descriptions and Objects. Sartre observes that Flaubert has a way of introducing descriptions just when something is about to happen. He "keeps us on the edge of the event" just long enough so that what finally happens seems somehow diminished. "It is the descriptions which prepare the event and annul it because they suggest to us that which makes us fall into revery." Landscape, he says, serve less as an environment for the characters than to refer us to a cosmic emptiness. They seem almost to annihilate persons and events. Sartre notes the several occasions in which Flaubert uses the word *vide* (empty) in describing his settings, usually for sky or meadow, once for Emma's room at Yonville. More specific descriptions emphasize the seeming inexhaustibility of what is observed. Sartre cites from Flaubert's letters a number of his comments concerning concrete objects. On first reading they might seem contradictory. Some of them indicate a fascination with things as they are in their separate, impenetrable existence. For example, "I know nothing more noble than the ardent comtemplation of the things of this world." The context of this remark is his professed admiration for science, but Sartre is probably right in assuming that Flaubert would hold the same attitude with respect to his writing. On another occasion we find, "Art is a representation: we must think only of representing." These and comparable passages would suggest that he thought of himself as the literary equivalent of a realist painter, a Courbet. Indeed, the challenge of conveying in words the quality of physical things always appealed to him as one worthy of the artist's powers. Other remarks suggest that it is not the object per se that is important but the subjective relationships imposed upon it. In a very late letter Flaubert writes, "Have you ever believed in the existence of things? Is not everything an illusion? What is true is only 'relations'; that is the way in which we perceive objects." And again, "The True does not exist. [*Il n'y a pas de Vrai.*] There are only ways of seeing. Is a photograph a resemblance? No more than an oil painting, or just as much." The use of the photograph as an example shows that the two sets of remarks are not really contradictory. For Flaubert any form of *mimesis* is a transformation of the real into the unreal, and this is precisely the artist's task. "Poetry is only a way of perceiving external objects, a special organ which filters the material and which, without changing it, transfigures it." Objects are the material out of which the imaginary world is created and made to appear real. But while Flaubert was interested in the problem of how style could be used to convey a quality impossible to express directly, the "taste of a plum pudding," for example, Sartre recognizes that descriptions in the novel are never there for their pictorial interest and only partially for the sake of guaranteeing versimilitude. In one of his notes Sartre sums up Flaubert's method by referring to music.

> All objects are nothing more than collected impressions ready
> to be modulated according to the rhythm of the sentence. . . .
> All things appear then as musical notes on which one will only
> have to compose the symphony, things which will be orches-
> trated into a totality, a correspondence between objects and
> minds which will make the very story, *this novel,* this poem.

This purpose of descriptions is aesthetic, of course, but it is half-philo-
sophical as well. They do not represent the focus of the characters' attention, but are a means whereby the author directs the reader's response.

> [Description] becomes for Flaubert the unique experience by
> which it seems possible to express the movements of life. It is
> analysis and expression of feelings which things symbolize, or
> support, the two being confused with one another. It is objects
> which carry the story insofar as they are seen by us, presented
> to arouse our emotion, our memories, and our revery.

Flaubert's use of objects as symbols has long been recognized. The cigar
case, the greyhound, Hippolyte's wooden leg, the statue of the curé which
breaks during the move from Toste to Yonville are among the most famous examples. My own favorite is the *Hirondelle,* the coach which first
brought Emma to Yonville, which took Léon away from her when he left
for Paris, which later carried her to him in Rouen. Its name, "The Swallow," is gently incongruous; it symbolizes ironically Emma's longing to
soar, to fly from banality to a world in which dreams are fulfilled without
travesty. The awakened memories, of which Sartre speaks, may refer to
connotations for the reader which come from outside the novel, but may
also be echoes of earlier passages. To give again an example of my own
choosing, there is Flaubert's use of Emma's parasol in two deliberately
contrasted passages in part one. The first occurs very early when Charles
still comes only as her father's physician. There is a thaw, everything is
melting.

> The parasol, of dove-colored shot silk through which the sun
> shone, lighted the white skin of her face with shifting hues. She
> smiled beneath the tender warmth; and drops of water were
> heard, falling one by one on the stretched silk.

Nothing is spoken, all is tender, warm, gentle; the tension is only of bur-
geoning promise. One day, after her marriage, Emma goes for a walk out
to a deserted pavilion. The walks are moldy, the shutters rotting on their
rusty bars, nettles surround the stones amid the remains of the garden. She

gives vent to her inward tension by making sharp jabs in the ground with the tip of her closed parasol and asks herself, "My God, why did I marry?" It is no accident that Emma carries her umbrella on both occasions.

Sartre lists a number of objects that add overtones of broken hopes, futility, despair by their reappearance in the story, e.g., the arbor, the greyhound, riding whips, and, of course, the bridal bouquet, the cigar case, and the mirror. He points to symbolic associations connected with levels in the house and with windows (borrowing here, I think, from Brombert's discussion of Flaubert's use of imagery). His more original contribution, however, concerns the extended descriptions of the physical environment. He claims that these are centrifugal, leading us away from the characters, forcing upon us a detachment that breaks our empathy with them, and introducing the chilling gaze of *le survol*. Unfortunately, Sartre himself has provided no example. Jonathan Culler, however, seems to have taken Sartre's lead and has provided substantial documentation for this immediate point of Sartre's, though Culler's ultimate conclusion as to why Flaubert's descriptions are as they are differs somewhat from Sartre's explanation.

From Flaubert's initial description of Yonville, Culler quotes two sentences which he feels "might well stand as touchstones of Flaubert's revolutionary achievement."

> The thatched roofs, like fur caps pulled down over the eyes, come down over a third of the low windows, whose bulging panes of old glass are decorated in the middle with a boss, like the bottoms of wine bottles. On the plaster wall, which is diagonally traversed by black beam-joists, a withered pear tree sometimes clings, and the ground floors have at their door a little swinging gate to keep out the chicks, which come to pick up, on the threshold, bits of wholemeal bread dipped in cider.

Culler, in a detailed analysis which I will not try to reproduce here, shows that these sentences are marked by three anomalies: first, their function is not truly grammatical. Especially in the first sentence he argues, "The point of arrival has nothing to do with the point of departure." Each sentence "appears to fritter itself away, as it runs down toward the minute and trivial." There is "no obvious thematic purpose." Second, "the sentences have no apparent function." They give us a collection of disparate facts. They tell us nothing to differentiate Yonville or to serve the story. Finally, the particularity of details suggests immediate and specific observation, but the mode is one of generalization—the withered pear tree that "sometimes clings," the chicks that regularly come to pick up the cider-soaked bread. No narrator seems to hold this all together. It is "a written text, which stands before us cut off from a speaker." Culler finds here the real meaning of Flaubert's impersonality. "One should always be in a position to claim that a description fell off a lorry." Or perhaps one has surreptitiously removed it, for Culler relates this notion to Sartre's claim that Flaubert's project was to "steal language from men."

Culler quotes a number of other passages from Flaubert's novels that show this same kind of movement "into inanity." Typically, the details in descriptions are presented without highlights to indicate what is important, almost in a flat listing. The piling up of items that are neither unified nor meaningful, that neither set a mood nor reveal a character, nor establish a definite perspective is certainly centrifugal, as Sartre says. Why is Flaubert so addicted to these descriptions? What purpose do they serve? One obvious answer Culler treats as obvious and rather unimportant. The impersonal, objective descriptions give a sense of reality.

> In so doing they reveal one of the basic conventions of post-seventeenth-century European culture: that "reality" is opposed to meaning. It consists of discrete concrete objects and events prior to any interpretation, and therefore to give a sense of "the real" one must offer details which have no meaning.

I would not dismiss the matter so quickly. It is hardly a convention of the last two and a half centuries that reality allows no human meanings to be imposed upon things. It has been the common assumption of novelists, confirmed recently by phenomenologists, that every one of us inhabits a "life world" overlaid with meaningful connections. To convey the quality of the world as lived by unique individuals has been a major concern of fiction writers. In reality, as Sartre has reminded us, one never encounters the material world without meanings—except abstractly. What is different about Flaubert is that he tries to look at the world as no individual, real or fictional, would ever look at it but rather as it would be seen by a nonhuman observer who comprehended human activities without sharing human interests. Culler understands this. The difference between his explanation of it and that given by Sartre comes out most clearly in his comment on Sartre's description of the Flaubert sentence.

Long before he had settled down to writing *The Family Idiot,* Sartre remarked on the peculiar deadening intent of Flaubert's style.

His sentence closes in upon the object, seizes it, immobilizes it, and breaks its back, wraps itself around it, changes into stone and petrifies the object along with itself. It is blind and deaf, bloodless, not a breath of life; a deep silence separates it from the sentence which follows; it falls into the void, eternally, and drags its prey down into that infinite fall. Any reality, once described, is struck off the inventory.

("What Is Literature?")

Opposing Sartre, Culler argues that the sentence does not actually destroy the object; rather, "The passivity of the sentence . . . suggests to us an unconcern with the objects which it goes beyond and leaves behind it as the jetsam of this formal quest." Herein lies the source of its charm for the reader, in Culler's opinion, and he says, "Calling attention to themselves as language, the sentences produce a discrepancy between novelistic signs and novelistic function." This is the essential point for Culler. Flaubert at all times wants to keep his readers alert to the fact that they are contemplating a work of art, not immersing themselves in life. Flaubert's novels "are novels" and must be "read as novels," Culler insists. "The novel is writing, not a world."

In contrast with Sartre, who says that *Madame Bovary* treats of two realities, Culler might say that it refuses to be about any reality. Yet Culler, like Sartre, recognizes that even in his persistent contrast between the novel and real life, Flaubert comments on the nature of our relation to the real. Consider the question of Charles Bovary's famous headpiece: Sartre, avoiding the elaborate allegorizing of some critics with regard to this ludicrous creation, says of it simply that its "mute ugliness has depths of expression. [It] is an image of Charles, and a sign alluding to his parents." Culler would avoid even this. He sees in this description the writer mocking his own enterprise as though searching for symbols which could not be found. "We follow the adventures of a language attempting to capture the world and make it signify but experiencing defeat before the particularity of an object about which one could go on and on without getting anywhere." Even if we were to say that Culler and not Sartre is right in this particular instance, I think myself that Flaubert is making a comment both on the limitations of language and reality. Culler would not necessarily deny this: LaCapra has criticized him for appropriating and developing Sartrean insights while contesting "Sartre's interpretive strategy." In my opinion, Culler, as much as any other critic in the period since *The Family Idiot* was published, has proved the fruitfulness of Sartre's work for Flaubertian studies. He explores, in a way that Sartre has not, some of the specific ways in which Flaubert has exploited "the uses of uncertainty" in narrative technique and in language itself. But he never denies that Flaubert's attitude toward the world and his personal project were divorced from his intentions in writing the novel. LaCapra, who is much more committed to contrasting Sartre's "totalizing dialectic" with a structuralist textual criticism, goes so far as to say that the fourth volume might have shown up the failure of the Sartrean method. "*Madame Bovary* as a text might have deconstructed the very type of discourse with which Sartre apparently would have tried to comprehend it." The view seems to me to rest on the mistaken belief that one can legitimately read a book by Flaubert as if it were written by Alain Robbe-Grillet or Michel Butor. To wish that one might write a book about nothing is not the same as to decide to write a work in which the text itself is the subject.

In the notes and earlier, too, Sartre indicated his intention of analyzing smaller units of Flaubert's sentences, especially verbs. He has emphasized especially Flaubert's extensive use of the passive voice and preference for iterative verbs and the imperfect tense. The passive voice, Sartre believes, reflects Flaubert's own personality as a "passive agent" and his propensity to see himself and others as victims of a "fatum," whether characterological or cosmic. Sartre has analyzed several passages in terms of tense usage, noting that Flaubert not only prefers the imperfect on occasions in which there is a clear choice between it and the simple past, but even on some occasions in which he is describing a single action or event. The effect, Sartre claims, is to suggest a feeling of endless and futile repetition, to deny temporality, to evoke "the ontological sense of life." In addition, Sartre had planned to include a comprehensive discussion of metaphors in a chapter on the processes of creative imagination. If he had been able to carry through successfully, he would have been able to demonstrate his argument and basic theme: that every line of *Madame Bovary,* if fully understood, would lead us back to Flaubert, the "singular individual" and the period that made and was modified by him. And we would have seen the first three volumes at the margin of every page of the fourth.

The Trial

Dominick LaCapra

> *La vérité sortira de l'examen sérieux du livre. [Truth will emerge from a serious examination of the book.]*
> SÉNARD for the Defense

> *Every notary carries within himself the debris of a poet.*
> FLAUBERT, *Madame Bovary*

How does the trial "read" the novel? Indeed how can a trial, given the framework in which it operates, read a novel? What sort of truth can emerge from the "serious examination" of a literary text at a trial?

One may initially approach these questions by attempting to specify the assumptions shared by the prosecution and the defense, for these were in crucial respects the conditions of possibility for the reading of the novel at the trial. Then one may look more closely at the arguments which led the two to opposite conclusions. Finally, one may examine the judgment of the court which, confronting problems peculiar to itself, indicated further difficulties in the reading at the trial. One may also note in passing that the trial followed a highly stylized format: the speech for the prosecution, the speech for the defense, and the judgment of the court. The monologues of the prosecution and the defense are of course marked by an internalized awareness of how the other might respond to certain points, and the court strains to arrive at some resolution of the issues in its decision. More direct dialogue is limited to a few brief interruptions or interjections on the part of the prosecutor during the speech of the defense. There is no direct questioning of witnesses or cross-examination in this judicial proceeding.

From Madame Bovary *on Trial*. © 1982 by Cornell University Press.

On one level, the prosecution and the defense share a great deal, and what they share is perhaps more important than what divides them. To be able to function in accordance with standard operating procedures, the trial had to rely on certain tacit assumptions which the novel both elicits and renders radically problematic. The trial does not, and perhaps cannot, explicitly recognize these assumptions or the way the novel treats them. All those participating in the trial—prosecution, defense, and the court in its judgment—tend to read the novel in an extremely restricted way. This reading is not simply wrong, for it is invited by one level on which the novel itself operates or functions: the level of conventional expectations about how things make sense. What does not register at the trial is the manner in which the novel renders this first level of understanding and expectation highly questionable in its world and, at least by implication, in the larger social world in which the trial takes place. Only at certain points, especially in the speech of the prosecutor, are these larger issues— issues that cannot be confined to conformity or deviance in relation to established norms—touched upon. At these points, the conventional framework of the trial itself threatens to explode, for then the question becomes that of the validity of the norms, categories, and criteria tacitly assumed by the trial as its basis of understanding and judgment. Here the standard relation between text and context tends to be reversed; it is no longer the context that provides determinate boundaries for interpreting and evaluating the text. Rather the text comes to challenge its context and the adequacy of its framing or boundary-marking devices, for it questions the viability of criteria of understanding and evaluation as they function within that context or others sufficiently analogous to it. What is of course not made evident at the trial is that, at these points, the issue can no longer be that of ordinary crime or failure to conform but must in some sense be that of political or "ideological" crime. The profound difficulty, however, is that "crime" of this sort is not amenable to more or less regular judicial proceedings because it contests the very right of the trial to judge it—and in ways that are extremely difficult to define, especially within the terms of a trial. If the challenge to the rules of the existing order is scandalous or disconcerting enough, scapegoating becomes an alluring option for those who wish to maintain that the established system is basically just. But so does the attempt to show that the challenge is not a challenge at all, since what constitutes a challenge may be construed as reinforcing the status quo. Thus one has the possibility that different conclusions will be reached by those who share the assumption that what exists is fundamentally legitimate.

The assumption that the society that forms the larger context for the novel is itself in a fundamentally healthy, normal, or legitimate state is, of course, never explicitly formulated or critically scrutinized at the trial. It constitutes the "unthought" ground of the trial—its unexamined preunderstanding of the nature of things through which the text is read. On its basis, the text may be understood and evaluated exclusively in terms of conformity to, or deviance from, established norms and values, for these norms and values are assumed to exist in a solid and unproblematic state within the larger sociopolitical and cultural context.

At the trial, the most significant explicit norms and values relate to the family and religion, and they permit one to draw a clear-cut opposition between marriage and adultery, the sacred and the profane. Since marriage is itself a sacrament in a Christian context, the two concerns may coalesce to give rise to the question of whether the novel conforms to, or deviates from, the image of the modern family as a holy family. In order that the novel may be processed in terms of this conventional but elevated "ideological" image, what must be more or less systematically suppressed, repressed, or avoided at the trial is the way *Madame Bovary* places in question the relevance of this image in the modern world and, with it, the fundamental assumptions about reading, understanding, and evaluation operative at the trial. Needless to add, the suppression of "evidence" in the novel for this kind of questioning cannot explicitly register at the trial. If it did register, those at the trial would be forced to engage in processes of self-reflection and self-criticism that would, to say the least, be difficult to accommodate within the parameters of the trial. For it becomes more difficult and complicated to judge when one senses that the grounds of judgment have become unstable. Indeed the very question of judgment tends to be displaced from the application of a standard in a case to the applicability of certain standards in a larger sociocultural context. A question of this sort does not facilitate standard operating procedures or routine processes of judgment. And chances are that it would be deemed irrelevant to the "normal" course of a trial. At this level, the trial and the novel may be at cross-purposes, or—to use a phrase of Karl Mannheim—the two may "talk past one another," because the differences are so extreme that they tend to jeopardize the existence of a common *habitus* or frame of reference in terms of which they may be adjudicated.

The fact that common assumptions structure the arguments of the prosecution and the defense often makes them appear as inverted mirror images of one another—almost like alter egos in a Flaubert novel. Discussion and decision turn on a simple binary choice of a positive or a negative answer to a set of shared questions. But there are a number of noteworthy variations in the way common assumptions and questions are employed, and it is worth mentioning them before treating in more detail the arguments of the prosecution and the defense.

The difference between the length of the speeches is the most obvious one. The prosecutor's speech covers nineteen pages of text in the Pléiade edition, while that of the defense attorney takes up forty-seven pages. The defense's presentation took over four hours to deliver, as Flaubert himself observed. The disproportionate size of the defense attorney's speech, along with what may have been a more effective mode of delivery, apparently gave it a greater rhetorical weight. A trial is one instance among numerous others in which oral presentation does make a difference. In the printed version of the trial, however, the prosecutor's speech appears to be more neatly argued, and it does succeed in raising a few points that even an attempted "critical" reading of the novel must confront.

Another difference between prosecution and defense is that between outrage and complacency. Sénard for the defense is unflappably complacent both in his thought and in his mode of presentation. He simply refuses to be bothered by certain questions. His interpretation is in one sense more narrowly conservative than that of the prosecutor, for—despite his apparently "liberal" conclusion—he construes the novel as a simple, clear, and distinct confirmation of existing morality and society. For Sénard, the author-narrator is a fully reliable guide in telling the sorry tale of Emma Bovary's fall and deserved punishment. The intention or spirit informing the novel is unmistakably one of moral condemnation attesting to the full rectitude of the narrator's (and the reader's) position. Only at rare points, which he does not notice, does Sénard's argument raise problems for the frame of reference in which it comfortably takes shape. Morality for Sénard is virtually identical with the existing order of society, and the moral of the novel is for him one of conservative adaptation within the status quo.

The relevant context for Pinard is Christian morality which is seen as the "foundation of modern civilizations." This view provides at least the possibility that existing society may deviate from its moral and religious foundation. Pinard himself does not note this implication or draw conclusions from it. He is concerned only with the presumed deviation of Flaubert's novel. But his sense of outrage at the enormity of this deviation threatens at times to carry him beyond the restricted framework of conformity or deviance vis-à-vis established and socially contextualized norms and values. He can be shocked by certain aspects of the novel that the defense attorney must try to interpret in fully conventionalizing terms.

A further difference may be mentioned in a preliminary way. Pinard's understanding of the intention or "thought" of the author is in keeping with his focus upon the text of the novel. For him, intention is fully "embodied": it is what the author means to say in the text. Pinard will supplement this concern by a brief appeal to a fragment of another text by Flaubert, *The Temptation of Saint Anthony,* only to find in it the same "color" as that which prevails in *Madame Bovary.* (This "lascivious" color brings about the demoralization of the reader.) The defense, by contrast, understands intention in a broader and less discriminating way, for it merges in his account with general questions of motivation and character. Indeed the defense will turn to the text of *Madame Bovary* only toward the very end of his speech, and at that point his understanding of it is entirely predetermined by his prior discussion of its authorial and literary lineage—its "precedents" in biography or sources and its status in the eyes of reputable character witnesses who are not questioned but invoked. For both the prosecution and the defense, reading and evaluation are very much constitutive of a *procès d'intention,* and it is assumed that the functioning of the text is essentially identical with the intention or "thought" of the author.

A final difference bears upon the way Pinard and Sénard relate to Emma Bovary and see her role in the novel. Both assume that she is the central character and that the reader's relation to her will be one of identification or recognition. But for Pinard, she serves as a positive identity and thus lures the reader into the same temptations and immoral forms of behavior to which she succumbed. Emma herself is not so much a scapegoat of society as a temptress who gets her way with men and who dies for purely contingent reasons devoid of moral import. For him, the novel does not present her suicide as punishment for her immorality. One might almost say that, for Pinard, Emma should be more of a scapegoat than she is, for she gets away with too much. For Sénard, Emma serves as a negative identity, providing the reader with an object (and an abject) lesson in what he or—more decidedly—she must avoid. She is a scapegrace who fully gets what she deserves.

Pinard and Sénard tend to become two more of Emma's men, and their drastically opposed but largely unqualified judgments concerning the way Emma is presented in the novel are in concert with their approaches to reading *Madame Bovary* as a whole. Another variation, however, occurs in this respect as well. Pinard will assume the role of the reader, but he will never directly assume that of the author—although he will interpret the novel as a function of his own understanding of the author's true "thought." Sénard blends the role of the reader and a rhetorical identification with that of the author, and he will even go so far as either to speak in the author's voice or to become a somewhat paternal underwriter or patron of Flaubert. Pinard thus identifies with Emma in ambivalent revulsion but refuses direct identification with Flaubert; Sénard refuses identification with Emma but securely substitutes himself for Flaubert.

Pinard begins his prosecution by noting a difficulty that he does not wish to dissimulate. The charge of offense to public morality and religion is "a little vague and a little elastic, and it is necessary to specify it." But this is not the difficulty that concerns him, for "upright and practical minds" will find it "easy to reach an understanding in this respect." The difficulty is rather that this charge is brought against "a novel in its entirety." A novel of some length, published in six installments in a periodical, poses problems distinct from those of an article that may readily be read to the court. The only solution in the case of a long work is "to narrate [raconter] the entire novel without reading from it" and then to incriminate the novel by quoting passages from the text. Thus Pinard justifies the method of paraphrase and synoptic content analysis, subsequently illustrated by quotation, by pointing to a simple difficulty in reading. He must replace Flaubert's extended narration with his own more condensed or economical one.

Pinard's next step is to query the title in the attempt to arrive at the text's core or synoptic meaning. The title and subtitle provided by Flaubert—*Madame Bovary: Moeurs de province*—do not, for him, explain the "thought" of the author; only the subtitle gives a presentiment of it. The author wanted to provide tableaux or pictures: the language of the novel is a "picturesque" one, and it depends upon the "colors" of the picture for its effects. While the portrait of the husband begins and ends the novel, "it is evidently [the portrait] of Madame Bovary" that is the most "serious" one in the novel, the one that "illuminates" all the others. For Pinard, Emma is the sun of this literary system.

Pinard then proceeds to a plot summary following the outline of the four principal scenes he will later use as frames for his quotations: (1) Emma's "fall" with Rodolphe, (2) the religious transition between the two adulteries, (3) the "fall" with Léon, (4) the death of Emma. On the basis of this summary, he feels justified in offering a new title, a précis of the novel's meaning, and a delineation of its dominant "color."

The new and more accurate title is "The History of the Adulteries of a Provincial Woman." The essential meaning is also the essential charge against the novel: "The offense to public morality is in the lascivious tableaux that I shall place before your eyes; the offense to religious morality is in the voluptuous images mingled with sacred things." The "general color of the author . . . is the lascivious color, before, during, and after the falls." The author, employing "all the wonders of his style," has used these colors to paint Madame Bovary, and the result is a glorification of adultery and and an undermining of marriage. For "the beauty of Madame Bovary is a beauty of provocation."

The genre or school to which this use of language belongs is the "realistic" one: "the genre which Monsieur Flaubert cultivates, that which he realizes without the circumspection of art but with all the resources of art, is the descriptive genre: it is realistic painting." Realism for Pinard seems to signify all that is upsetting in the art of Flaubert. But it is more specifically related to Flaubert's presumably "lascivious" colorations and to his lack of *mesure* or circumspection in art. Pinard will hark back to these complaints in his conclusion. At this point, he asserts that the fragments of *The Temptation of Saint Anthony* printed in the review, *L'Artiste,* reveal the same "color," the same "energy of the brush," and the same "vivacity of expression" as *Madame Bovary*.

In developing his argument, Pinard interrupts a quotation to interject a parenthetical expression of scandalized dismay. The phrase over which he stumbles and whose peculiar nature he senses is: *"les souillures du mariage et les désillusions de l'adultère"* [the defilements of marriage and the disillusions of adultery]. He notices the telling reversal of ordinary expectations that Flaubert effects with this phrase. "There are those who would have said: 'The disillusions of marriage and the defilements of adultery.' " And shortly thereafter, he repeats this complaint and adds: "Often when one is married, instead of the unclouded happiness one expected, one encounters sacrifices and bitterness. The word disillusion might be justified; that of defilement could never be."

The effect of the novel on the reader—and perhaps the intention of the author—is for Pinard one of demoralization and corruption. The novel is literally poison. It is especially dangerous for its most probable readership:

> Who will read the novel of Monsieur Flaubert? Will it be men who busy themselves with political or social economy? No! The light pages of *Madame Bovary* will fall into even lighter hands—into the hands of young women, sometimes of married women. Well, when the imagination will have been seduced, when seduction will have descended into the heart, when the heart will have spoken to the senses, do you believe that a very

cold reasoning will be very strong against this seduction of the senses and of sentiment? In addition, even men must not drape themselves too much in their force and virtue; men too harbor instincts from below and ideas from above and, with everyone alike, virtue is the consequence of effort, very often painful effort. Lascivious paintings generally have more influence than cold reasonings.

Pinard thus restages a very old conflict in almost storybook fashion. The cold light of reason is weak in comparison with the heat of the imagination and passion. The language of art is the language of images and pictures that appeal to the lower faculties. The fatal declension from the imagination to the senses that it effects is especially dangerous for women, who are particularly prone to its allures. But men themselves may be feminized by literature, and their protective garments may be penetrated by its wiles. Man as he reads literature must also be provided with a safeguard to supplement his "force and virtue." Here one has the proper province of the laws as guardians of public morality and religion.

Drawing to a close, Pinard attempts to preempt an important line of defense. "One will say as a general objection: but, after all, the novel is fundamentally moral, because adultery is punished." For Pinard, even if the ending were moral, it would still not justify "lascivious" details in the book; if it did, anything would be justified by a moral ending. But even assuming that this end existed—an assumption Pinard denies—it would not justify the means. For "this would go against the rules of common sense. It would amount to putting poison in the reach of all and the antidote in the hands of a very small number, if indeed there were an antidote."

The ending of *Madame Bovary* is not truly moral for Pinard. The death of Emma proves nothing. There is no moral connection between her adultery and death such that the latter counts as warranted punishment for the former. "She dies not because she is adulterous but because she wanted to die. She dies in all the splendor of youth and beauty." Thus the poisoning of Madame Bovary is itself no antidote to the poisoning of the reader brought about the way Emma and adultery are painted. Her self-poisoning is a willful event that resembles her adultery, thereby compounding her crime rather than serving as a punishment for it.

Pinard concludes with general reflections on the immorality of the novel "from a philosophical point of view." Touching upon what later theorists would refer to as unreliable narration, he exclaims:

Who can condemn this woman in the book? Nobody. Such is
the conclusion. There is not in the book a character who can
condemn her. If you find in it a wise character, if you find in
it a single principle in virtue of which adultery may be stigmatized then I'm wrong. Thus if in all the book there is not a character who can make her bend her head; if there is not an idea,
a line in virtue of which adultery is scourged, then I am right:
the book is immoral. . . . Would you condemn her in the name
of the author's conscience? I do not know what the author's
conscience thinks.

Thus for Pinard there is no stable, secure, or reliable position within
the novel from which to condemn Emma. Conjugal honor is represented
by a benighted husband who literally hands his wife over to her lovers.
Public opinion is "personified in a grotesque being, the pharmacist Homais, who is surrounded by ridiculous people whom this woman dominates." Religious sentiment is incarnated in the priest Bournisien, "a priest
about as grotesque as the pharmacist, believing only in physical and never
moral suffering, almost a materialist." The author is an elusive presence at
best whose position cannot be determined. What is left is the overpowering personality of Emma and the example she gives. Within the novel,
"the only personage who dominates is Madame Bovary."

For Pinard the fact that no one in the novel is in a position to throw
the first stone leads to the conclusion that one must look outside the text
to a larger and more certain text—that of "Christian morality, which is the
foundation of our modern civilizations." In the light of the higher morality cast by this more certain sun, "everything becomes explained and clari-
fied." For this morality serves as the source of clear and absolute principles
through which the novel and its characters may be judged. It alone is a
force able to dominate Emma Bovary and put an end to her poisonous
influence.

In its name adultery is stigmatized and condemned not because
it is an imprudence which exposes one to disillusionments and
regrets but because it is a crime for the family. You stigmatize
and condemn suicide not because it is an act of madness—the
madman is not responsible, not because it is an act of coward-
ice—it at times demands a certain physical courage, but because
it is the contempt for one's duty in the life which is ending and
a cry of disbelief in the life that begins. This morality stigma-

tizes realistic literature not because it paints the passions: hatred, vengeance, love—the world lives on nothing else, and art must paint them—but when it paints them without brakes, without measure [*mésure*]. Art without rules is no longer art; it is like a woman who takes off all her clothes. To impose upon art the unique rule of public decency is not to subordinate it but to honor it. One can grow only in accordance with a rule. These are the principles which we profess; this is a doctrine which we defend conscientiously.

Before turning from Pinard's forcefully imperious peroration to Sénard's defense, one may note an aspect of Pinard's argument to which Sénard does not respond for obvious reasons. It concerns degrees of guilt among author, publisher, and printer, and it casts an interesting light upon Pinard's conception of liability in publication.

For Pinard, the publisher and the printer have a second-order responsibility, and one may show a certain leniency toward them. The publisher Pichat is to be held accountable not because he suppressed a few passages but because he should have suppressed more. The printer is placed by Pinard in a crucial position: "he is the advance sentinel against scandal." Printers must read what they print, and if they fail to read or to have others read what they commit to paper, they do so at their own risk and peril. "Printers are not machines; they have a privilege; they take an oath; they are in a special situation; and they are responsible." As advance sentinels, "if they let an infraction pass, it is as if they had let the enemy pass." But it is above all Flaubert who is "the principal culprit: for him the court must reserve all its severity." Those with lesser degrees of responsibility may benefit from mitigating circumstances, but no mercy should be shown to the author whose responsibility is absolute.

Sénard's defense takes the tack that Pinard's sense of outrage is entirely misplaced. For the novel is not at all sacrilegious or nonconformist. On the contrary, it is the fully reputable and responsible confirmation of conventional morality.

Sénard begins by giving his own rendition of the intention or thought of the author. It is "an eminently moral and religious thought that can be translated by these words: the incitement to virtue through horror of vice [*l'incitation à la vertu par l'horreur du vice*]." It is, however, curious that in striking his first note, Sénard seems to introduce a little dissonance. "Incitement" is a strange word to apply to virtue, for it is a word that would ordinarily be applied to vice. Indeed it is a rather "passionate" word. Sénard himself seems to get involved initially in a reversal of ordinary expectations that might be seen as an unintentional mimesis of Flaubert, for his phrase resembles Flaubert's *"les souillures du mariage et les désillusions de l'adultère."* Sénard's magisterial speech is not caught up by such a bagatelle. Indeed he does not notice any problem. His entire line of defense is one of insistent conventionalization of the novel, conducted with all the confirmed skill of forensic rhetoric. *Madame Bovary* becomes in his hands a provincial *Bildungs-roman* or a *roman à thèse* leading on all levels to a resounding reaffirmation of existing morality and society.

Sénard engages Pinard in a battle of titles and the right thereto. He vehemently protests against Pinard's proposed subtitle for the novel. His own counter-title requires rather lengthy exposition of his understanding of the novel's essential meaning:

> No! The second title of this work is not *The Story of the Adulteries of a Provincial Wife;* it is, if you absolutely must have a second title, the story of the education too often given in the provinces; the story of the dangers to which it can lead; the story of degradation, of villainy, of a suicide seen as a consequence of an early transgression, and of a transgression that was itself induced by a first misstep into which a young woman is often led; it is a story of an education, the story of a deplorable life to which this sort of education is too often the preface.

Madame Bovary becomes in Sénard's presentation the story of social maladjustment: a farmer's daughter, socially predestined to become the wife of a small-town *officier de santé,* receives an education inappropriate for her station in life. This discrepancy between social position and the illegitimate expectations created by education is the source of Emma's difficulties, and the lesson Sénard draws from it is socially and morally conservative.

> Oh! God knows, those of our young women who do not find enough in honest and elevated principles or in a strict religion to keep them steadfast in the performance of their duties as mothers, who do not find it above all in that resignation, that practical understanding of life that tells us that we must make the best of what we have, but who turn their reveries outside, these most honorable and pure young women who, in the prosaic everydayness of their household, are sometimes tormented by what goes on around them—a book like this will, you can

be sure, lead more than one of them to reflect. This is what
Monsieur Flaubert has done. . . . The dénouement in favor of
morality is found in every line of the book.

Indeed, for Sénard, every line of the book poses the question: "Have
you done all you should in the education of your daughters?" To establish
the exemplary morality of the novel, Sénard begins with an extensive discussion of Flaubert's character and family. "M. Gustave Flaubert is a man
with a serious character, carried by his nature toward grave and serious
things." His studies, "conforming to the nature of his spirit," were also
serious and large, and "they included not only all branches of literature but
also the law." (Given Flaubert's intense hatred of his early legal studies,
the last point is an especially nice touch.)

The defense of Flaubert is for Sénard a matter both of conscience and
of friendship. Flaubert's father was his friend, and the good doctor's honorable son is the friend of Sénard's children.

> His illustrious father was for more than thirty years surgeon-
> in-chief at the Hôtel Dieu of Rouen. He was the protector of
> Dupuytren. In giving his great teachings to science, he en-
> dowed it with great men of whom I need only cite a single
> one—Cloquet. He has not only himself left a great name to sci-
> ence, he has left great memories of immense services rendered
> to humanity.

Thus Sénard establishes an impressive genealogy of moral respectability for his client. But he is himself the principal character witness, and he
postulates both a personal responsibility for Flaubert's text and a privileged
access to the mind of the author enabling him to speak in Flaubert's voice.
He attempts to generate the most traditional kind of patron–client relationship between himself and the author of *Madame Bovary:* "I know his
thought; I know his intentions; and the lawyer has the right to present
himself as the personal bondsman [or bail—*caution*] for his client."

Along with a personal genealogy, Sénard will also establish a literary
lineage of impeccable respectability to which Flaubert is the rightful heir.
From character references concerning the person of the author, he turns to
precedents and opinions assuring the moral quality of the text. Flaubert's
sources included not only past masters such as Bossuet and Massillon but
(with reference to the scene of Emma's Extreme Unction) the *Rituel* of the
Catholic Church itself. Indeed Sénard's ploy will be to attempt to show
that the most unquestionably canonized of precedents in the literary tradi-

tion are more daring and explicit than *Madame Bovary* in treating the theme of sex. Far from being lascivious or *outre mesure,* the text is exceedingly chaste; it is also less disconcerting than the most anodyne classics in the Western heritage.

Early in his defense, Sénard mentions the phrase which caused Pinard difficulties: the seeming reversal of ordinary expectations in *"les souillures du mariage et les désillusions de l'adultère."* Sénard's strategy is to pass quickly over the first part of the phrase and to avoid the problem of reversal altogether. Instead he dwells on the second part of the phrase in pacified isolation, and he provides a thoroughly reassuring gloss of it, construing it as a testimony to the way in which adultery will not bring a hoped-for escape from the platitudes of marriage but only something worse:

> There where you expected to find love, you will find only libertinage. There where you expected to find happiness, you will find only bitterness. A husband who goes quietly about his affairs, who puts on his nightcap and eats his supper with you, is a prosaic husband who disgusts you. You dream of a man who loves you, who idolizes you, poor child! That man will be a libertine who will have taken you up for a moment to play with you. . . . The man of whom you dreamed will have lost all his glamour; you will have rediscovered in love the platitudes of marriage, and you will have rediscovered them with contempt and scorn, with disgust and piercing remorse.

This apostrophe to Emma is intended to show how the novel brings out her foolishness and bad judgment.

Sénard peremptorily rejects Pinard's understanding of the genres or literary movements to which the text belongs. For him the novel is quite intelligible on grounds of common sense and without appeal to special categories of interpretation:

> What is the frame he has chosen, what is his subject, and how has he treated it? My client is a person who belongs to none of the schools whose names I have just heard in the indictment. My God! He belongs to the realist school only in the sense that he is interested in the real nature of things. He belongs to the psychological school in the sense that he is prompted, not by the materiality of things, but by human sentiment and the development of passions in a given milieu. He belongs to the romantic school perhaps less than any other, for if romanticism

does appear in his book, just as realism appears, it is only in a few ironic phrases, scattered here and there, which the public ministry has taken too seriously. What Monsieur Flaubert wanted above all was to take a subject of study from real life and to create or constitute true middle-class types, thereby arriving at a useful result. Yes, what has most preoccupied my client in this study to which he had dedicated himself is precisely this useful purpose, and he has pursued it by setting forth three or four characters from present-day society living in real-life circumstances, and by presenting to the reader's eye a true tableau of what most often happens in the world.

As Hans Robert Jauss has noted, Sénard here touches upon the "mistake" of the prosecuting attorney in attributing opinions or views in passages written in the "free indirect style" directly to the author ("Literary History as a Challenge to Literary Theory"). But the principal thrust of Sénard's comments is to show that the realism of the novel is a garden variety subordinated to a higher utilitarian purpose. The effect of the work on readers—especially that delicate class of readers referred to by Pinard—can only be a beneficial one. Sénard rhetorically asks: "Can this book, placed in the hands of a young girl, have the effect of drawing her toward easy pleasures, toward adultery, or will it on the contrary show the danger of the initial steps and make her tremble with horror?" He later more than answers his question.

My God! [a favorite exclamation of Sénard] There are nuances which may sometimes escape us given our habits, but they cannot escape women of great intelligence, of great purity, of great chastity. There are names that cannot be pronounced before the court, but if I were to tell you what has been said to Monsieur Flaubert, what has been said to me by mothers of families who read the book.

Thus the weak and susceptible vessels of Pinard become for Sénard the exemplary recipients of the novel's true message. And Sénard does proceed to tell the court of the reaction of one reader special in his eyes—a highly poetical and sensitive man.

Nevertheless, among all these literary opinions there is one I wish to tell you of. Among them is a man respected for a fine and noble character, a man who fights courageously each day against adversity and suffering, a man famous not only for many deeds unnecessary to recall here, but famous as well for his literary works, which we must recall, for therein lies his authority—an authority all the greater for the purity and chasteness that exist in all his writings—Lamartine.

Lamartine was not acquainted with my client; he was unaware that he existed. Lamartine, at home in the country, had read *Madame Bovary* as it was published in each number of the *Revue de Paris*. Lamartine's impressions were so strong that they grew even greater with the events that I now describe. ·

After this initial flourish of epideictic oratory, Sénard proceeds to tell a somewhat expurgated version of the story of how Lamartine sent for Flaubert and told him of his admiration for *Madame Bovary,* omitting Lamartine's failure to provide a promised letter to be used at the trial and the plausible grounds for this failure. For Lamartine's was precisely the type of "romantic" work used ironically and parodically in *Madame Bovary.* (As Flaubert, who was nonetheless upset by Lamartine's failure to keep his word about the promised letter, wrote on January 25, 1857: "It was Lamartine who initiated the courtesies: that surprises me considerably—I would never have expected the bard of Elvire to conceive a passion for Homais." Lamartine appears in Flaubert's letters as an exemplar of the most saccharine romanticism.) But Sénard does, in bathetic tones, tell of Lamartine's one reservation about the novel—a reservation presumably attesting to Flaubert's moral rigor: "Lamartine only added: At the same time that I read you without reservation down to the last page, I reproached you for the last ones. You hurt me, you literally made me suffer! The expiation is literally out of proportion to the crime; you have created a frightful, a hideous death!"

Sénard also informs the court that he has with him a "portfolio filled with opinions about the book in question by all the literary writers of our time, including the most distinguished, expressing the admiration they felt on reading this new work that is at once so moral and so useful."

Given this account of the indubitably moral character of the novel, Sénard felt obliged to offer some explanation of the seemingly incredible fact that the work could ever have induced litigation. His own defense threatened to be self-defeating, for it made the legal system seem implausibly inept and foolish—almost like one of the more grotesque beings in Flaubert's novel. The explanation he offers is similar to that of many later commentators whose primary source of information he may well be. For he sees the grounds of trial as being almost entirely circumstantial. Thus the idea that the novel was a mere pretext arises in an apparent attempt of the defense attorney to explain away the problem of why Flaubert was placed on trial in the first place.

Sénard recounts that the excision of the scene in the fiacre or cab during the printing of the first installment of *Madame Bovary* led Flaubert to insist that the direction of the *Revue de Paris* insert a note explaining that they saw fit to suppress a passage.

> Well! This unhappy suppression is [the cause of] the trial, that is, in the offices charged, with infinitely good reason, to exercise surveillance over all writings that might offend against public morality, when they saw this cut, it put them on the alert. [The jumbled construction of this sentence by the usually careful Sénard may be significant here.] In those offices, they said: We must watch out for what comes next; when the following issue appeared, they fought over every syllable. These officials are not obliged to read everything, and when they saw it written that a woman had removed all her clothes, they took alarm without going any further.

On the basis of this partially fictionalized reconstruction of the censor's reaction and in view of what he sees as an "excess of reserve" that induced precensorship on the part of the *Revue de Paris,* Sénard sees fit to read the entire fiacre scene to the court. The reading of "this fantastic ride" is to show how its excision gave rise to false expectations about its real content. People expected "something analogous to what you will be kind enough to read in one of the most marvelous novels to come from the pen of an honorable member of the French Academy, Monsieur Mérimée." In *La Double Méprise,* Mérimée—in marked contrast to Flaubert—describes what goes on inside a cab, and he does so in terms that prevent Sénard from reading the passage aloud in court. And, aside from references to the poetry of André Chenier and *Les Lettres Persanes* of Montesquieu, Sénard tells the court that he has an entire collection of passages from the greats that make *Madame Bovary* seem prudish by comparison. Thus, far from liberating art from all rules and restraints, Flaubert has more *pudeur* than acknowledged and revered masters of the past.

The reading of the fiacre scene heralds Sénard's long deferred turn from character references, precedents, and context to the text itself. "The public ministry attacks the book; I must take up the book itself in order to defend it. I must complete the quotations he has made, and for each passage I must show the nullity of the accusation. This will be my whole defense."

Sénard's procedure will be to argue that the prosecution quoted out of context and that his own response will simply be to quote more fully and in context. He alludes to his project of publishing with Flaubert a *Mémoire* that he himself would have signed with the author, composed of an annotated version of the entire text of *Madame Bovary*. Thus he was ready to underwrite with the authority of his own signature his belief in the respectability of the text. But an injunction was directed against the explanatory notes. Left with the text alone to defend, Sénard declares that he will not appeal to the "elevated, animated, and pathos-ridden appreciations" of the prosecutor. He will simply "cite the texts just as they are." Sénard's earlier discussion of "extratextual" considerations had, of course, functioned to prefigure his discussion of the text. His exegesis will hold no surprises, for it will amount to variations on the theme of the novel's moral excellence. Indeed he immediately offers his overall understanding of the way the text will speak for itself. "First of all, I declare that nothing is more false than what was earlier said about the lascivious color." Nothing in the book warrants this designation—neither the portrait of Emma nor the depiction of religion. To illustrate the way the novel has a salutary influence in revealing the dangers of the manner in which religion is often presented to the young, Sénard offers his own reactions as criteria of reader response. He does so in terms that both replicate the prosecutor's sentiments and go even further in providing what might be seen as an unself-conscious parody of Homais's own parody of Rousseau's Profession of Faith of a Savoyard Vicar:

> As for myself, here is what I flatly declare: I know of nothing more beautiful, more useful, and more necessary to support us in the path of life [than religion]: not only for women, but also for men, who themselves have at times extremely painful trials to overcome. I know of nothing more useful and necessary, but the religious sentiment must be solemn and, allow me to add, it must be severe. I want my children to understand God, not a God in the abstractions of pantheism, but a Supreme Being with whom they are in harmony, to whom they raise themselves in prayer, and who, at the same time, helps them to grow and gives them strength.

(Compare Homais who may here perhaps be credited with a greater frankness:

> I have a religion, my religion, and I even have more than all these others with their mummeries and their juggling. I adore

God, on the contrary. I believe in the Supreme Being, in a Creator, whatever he may be. I care little who has placed us here
below to fulfill our duties as citizens and parents; but I don't
need to go to church to to kiss silver plates, and fatten out of
my pocket, a lot of good-for-nothings who live better than we
do. For one can know him as well in a wood, in a field, or even
contemplating the ethereal heavens like the ancients. My God is
the God of Socrates, of Franklin, of Voltaire, and of Béranger! I
support the *Profession de Foi du Vicaire savoyard* and the immor-
tal principles of '89! And I can't admit an old boy of a God who
takes walks in his garden with a cane in his hand, who lodges
his friends in the belly of whales, dies uttering a cry, and rises
up again at the end of three days; things absurd in themselves,
and completely opposed, moreover, to all physical laws, which
proves to us, by the way, that priests have always wallowed in
squalid ignorance, and tried to drag whole nations down after
them.)

Filling thirty pages in the Pléiade edition, Sénard engages the prosecutor in a war of quotations, and he clearly marshals the bigger battalions.
As he mounts quote upon quote, his method of identifying himself with
the voice of the author at times goes to histrionic extremes: "Ah! You
have accused me of confounding the religious element with sensualism in
my picture of modern society! Rather accuse the society in which we live;
do not accuse the man who like Bossuet, cries out: 'Awake and beware of
the danger.' "

As Sénard literally becomes Flaubert's mouthpiece, one might notice
a possible breach or diversion in his argument. The question of the manner
in which the novel "accuse[s] the society in which we live" might lead to
the problem of ideological crime. But this implication is not pursued, and
the reference to society remains purely rhetorical in Sénard's presentation.
Indeed the process of filling out the prosecutor's quotations can, for Sénard, lead inevitably to only one conclusion: "The reading of this book cannot produce in you an impression other than that which it produced in
us, that is, that this book is excellent as a whole and that its details are
irreproachable."

The verdict of the court constitutes a very weak dénouement to the
trial. The Aristotelian might find it a highly implausible ending to the
case. For the argument of the court seems up until the last minute to con-
cur forcefully with the views of the prosecutor. But then an anticlimatic

turning point is reached, and the court refuses to draw the apparent conclusion. Instead, almost in an incongruous aside, Flaubert is reprieved.

In the words of the court, Flaubert's work does "deserve stern censure, for the mission of literature must be to enrich and to refresh the spirit
by improving the understanding and by perfecting the character, more
than to instill a loathing of vice by offering a picture of the disorders that
may exist in society." Indeed "it is not permitted, under pretext of painting local color, to reproduce in all their immorality the exploits and say-
ings of the characters the writer has made it his duty to paint, . . . such a
system applied to the works of the mind as well as to the products of the
fine arts would lead to a realism that would be the negation of the beautiful and the good, and that, in begetting works equally offensive to sight
and mind, would be committing continual outrages against public morality and decency." Thus, for the court, the ideal and idealizing function of
art itself condemns the putative "realism" practiced by Flaubert. What is
significant is that the court itself affirms a stereotypically Platonic conception of art in order to censure Flaubert and, by implication, all "realists."
In so doing, it provides evidence for the view that the official aesthetic ide-
ology of the time was idealistic. Flaubert, in the eyes of the court, has "insufficiently understood" that "there are limits that even the most frivolous
literature must not overstep." But the court nonetheless concludes that the
charges against Flaubert have been insufficiently proved, not explaining
how its own seemingly absolute judgments can be converted into a matter
of degree. Evidence of rather nominal acquiescence by the author in the
rituals of established society seems to be enough for the court. It is content
to observe that Flaubert's novel was the product of much work, that the
author affirms his respect for decency, and that his sole aim was not the
gratification of the passions. "He has committed only the fault of sometimes losing sight of the rules that no self-respecting writer should ever
infringe and of forgetting that literature, like art, if it is to achieve the good
that it is called upon to produce, must be chaste and pure not only in its
form but in its expression." Thus the court will reprimand Flaubert, make
him sit through a didactic lecture on art (in other circumstances a sufficient
punishment for Flaubert), and release him without awarding him the costs
of the trial.

Narrative Strategies in *Madame Bovary*

Michal Peled Ginsburg

In the first version of the *Tentation,* the narrator and his surrogate Antoine disappeared—"died"—and gave their places to a spectacle that faced them as an independent reality. The citational character of the work, its rhetorical order, the conventional, cliché nature of the visions, the emphasis on the problem of incarnation—all contributed to making Antoine a passive and empty figure. In the person of Antoine, the self does not express its original, individual desires through language, but instead is seen as predetermined and passively manipulated by a world of discourse that is exterior and anterior to it. In contrast to the *Mémoires* or *Novembre,* where the narration repeatedly reached a narcissistic impasse and had to stop and start afresh (using each time a new mode of narration), the text of the first *Tentation* flows without interruption and without end: the difficulty in generating the text has been overcome. But this textual richness is accompanied by a psychological poverty; the superabundance of the text is counterbalanced by the emptiness of the self whose story the text is supposed to recount.

How does this analysis of the early works contribute to our understanding of *Madame Bovary*? Of all the works of Flaubert, *Madame Bovary* is the one that has always invited analysis in terms of the entire oeuvre. The first of his works to be published and to enjoy recognition, it has always been acclaimed as the first "mature" work, with maturity understood as a break with his previous, so-called romantic view of life and art. Possibly the reason for this view of maturity is to be found within *Madame*

Bovary itself, where characters (Charles or Léon, for example) outgrow romantic, "poetic" dreams and accept prosaic (novelistic, bourgeois) reality. Charles and Léon can thus be seen as deliberate, though ironic, self-portraits. But the parallel evolution of characters and author suggests another possibility: if, as I assume is agreed, characters in a novel "grow" according to narrative constraints, then the process of "embourgeoisement" is in fact determined by narrative rather than socio-cultural pressure. Can we not then interpret the development of Flaubert's work—that is to say, the passage from the first *Tentation* to *Madame Bovary*—in the same terms? On this interpretation *Madame Bovary* and Flaubert's realism in general could be seen as growing out of the unsolved problems of the earlier works. In what follows I shall examine *Madame Bovary* from this particular point of view—as an attempt to remedy the central flaw of the first *Tentation*. I will claim that where the first version of the *Tentation,* following the first *Education sentimentale,* tried to circumvent the narcissistic impasse, *Madame Bovary* attempts to generate a narration by accepting and radicalizing the narcissistic predicament in order to save a self, even if it is an imaginary one. Instead of beginning a new mode of narration, as most critics claim it does, *Madame Bovary* marks a return—with important modifications, to be sure—to the early works.

Madame Bovary can be interpreted as an elaboration of those scenes in Flaubert's early works in which the narrator, having eliminated the all-too-menacing mirror image, tries to create a story around a specter that replaces it. Like that specter, Emma is an imaginary character: a character whose life, desire and even body are created and shaped by others. Never allowed to gain life and independence, she remains a character deprived of the capacity to fully become a narrator.

The imaginary nature of Emma's existence can be understood in different but complementary ways. Most obviously, her existence is "doubly bookish" (Philippe Bonnefis, "Récit et histoire dans *Madame Bovary*"). Not only is she a fictive character in a book, but as a character—as a desiring subject—she has been created by literature: "And Emma tried to find out what one meant exactly in life by the words *bliss, passion, ecstasy,* that had seemed to her so beautiful in books" (Flaubert's emphasis); "Then she recalled the heroines of the books that she had read. . . . She became herself, as it were, an actual part of these imaginings." The theme of the dangers of reading, the corrupting influence of literature (a cliché theme, of course), is the most obvious expression of Emma's imaginary existence.

That a character's desire should be determined by a previous text is not in itself something new in Flaubert. We saw this happen in both the early works and the first version of the *Tentation*. But in the early works the nonoriginality of desire was recognized and felt as a menace (by the narrator-hero of the *Mémoires* or *Novembre,* by the hero-artist Jules of the first *Education*), and in the *Tentation* it was exploited (by the narrator and his various surrogates) as a way of generating a text. What characterizes *Madame Bovary* and distinguishes it from those works is that Emma—unlike the narrator—is not aware of the borrowed nature of her desire. Her inability to see repetition, to recognize clichés as clichés—her blindness to the fact that her desire is the desire of the other—manifest her narcissism.

On the level of plot Emma's imaginary existence is conveyed by the fact that she is always seen and chosen—created as an object of desire—by others. As most critics have observed, in the first encounter between Emma and the various men who shape her life, we are not given Emma's point of view. Instead of a description of Charles, Léon, or Rodolphe as seen by Emma, we have a description of Emma as seen by the desiring eyes of Charles, Léon, or Rodolphe. We are not told what Emma's feelings, impressions, or desires are when she first meets these men. We are told of her feelings toward Charles only after the consummation of their marriage: "Before marriage she thought herself in love. . . . The uneasiness of her new position, or perhaps the disturbance caused by the presence of this man, had sufficed to make her believe that she at last felt that wondrous passion"; her love for Léon is described only when she realizes he loves her: "Looking from her bed at the bright fire that was burning, she still saw, as she had down there, Léon standing up. . . . She thought him charming; she could not tear herself away from him. . . . Is he not in love? she asked herself; but with whom? . . . with me!"; we get a glimpse of her feelings toward Rodolphe only at the end of the *Comices,* when, on hearing Rodolphe's words, "something gave way in her. . . . The sweetness of this sensation revived her past desires, and like grains of sand under a gust of wind, they swirled around in the subtle breath of the perfume that diffused over her soul." This fact of narrative technique should not be taken lightly; it means that in terms of the novel, Emma does not exist as a desiring subject before she is made such, first by literature, then by the men who choose her. (It is rather obvious, and important, that the literature Emma reads is written by men: among the authors mentioned or alluded to in the chapter dealing with her readings, we do not find Madame de Staël or Georges Sand, for example. The heroines of the novels Emma reads are the images of perfect femininity as conceived by men, in response to *their* desire. When Emma dreams of becoming like one of those heroines, she desires to become the ideal object of a man's desire.) Rather than being an autonomous subject whose desire originates within herself and whose consciousness of herself is independent of other people, Emma exists only as an object of desire created by the others (men and literature). This "inessentiality" is emphasized by her never being the "first one" for any of the men around her: she is Charles's second wife, one of many mistresses for Rodolphe, and Léon's only after he has lost his virginity to some working girl in Paris. She is not even the first victim of Lheureux (who shapes her life financially rather than erotically). Being second means filling in the place left by someone else, fitting into a preexisting slot. Just as the theme of reading shows that the self is produced by the order of language that precedes it and determines it, so the plot inscribes Emma in a circle of exchange where she is not an autonomous subject but an object of substitution.

Emma is, then, in spite of her hyperactivity, as passive as the Saint Antoine of the first version. His temptations, orchestrated by a medieval Devil, were the "clichés" of the old morality plays; her dreams, like his, are stereotypical and banal, and her "temptations"are always controlled by others. Why is it, then, that we feel that Emma is so different from Saint Antoine of the first version, that whereas he is an empty figure, a pretext for the unfolding of images, she is a real woman? The reason is that unlike Antoine, whose attention always moves from one image or temptation to the next without lingering too long on any of them, Emma "succumbs to temptation" and fixes her attention on successive single images.

In the first *Tentation* constant movement from one image to another, from one "possible life" to another, generated a text, but at the same time prevented it from being the story of a self. A self can come into being as a self (can have a story) only by arresting its attention on one image, fixing its flow at one "possible life." To have an identity, it must be narcissistic, must enter into an exclusive, specular relation with the image that its desire has created or that has created its desire. Emma, like Félicité of "Un Coeur simple" later on, repeatedly tries to anchor her shifting existence in a single image, be it Charles, Léon, Rodolphe, God, or Lagardy. But because the relation that constitutes her as a desiring self is specular and exclusive, its end means her death. Just as the narrator in the *Mémoires* or *Novembre* was shaped by the narcissistic cycle and therefore periodically reached an impasse, then had to stop and start afresh, so too in *Madame Bovary* Emma's life is punctuated by points of rupture, "little deaths," followed each time by a new departure.

But, again, Emma's particularity is her refusal to recognize the repetition in her life. A product of the desire of the other, a fragment in a chain of substitutions that constitutes her as a desiring subject, ironically she experiences each successive desire as something totally new, as something that has not happened before and cannot happen again—hence, as an "original" desire. On the one hand, every new lover is a totally new beginning, and it is as if nothing has existed before; on the other hand, all her lovers tend to collapse into a single image of a lover. "Then something gave way in her. . . . It seemed to her that she was again turning in the waltz under the light of the lustres on the arm of the Viscount, and that Léon was not far away, that he was coming . . . and yet all the time she was conscious of Rodolphe's head by her side." What Emma experiences each time as newness and originality is precisely what never stops repeating itself; it is the "virginity" of the prostitute in *Novembre*—the inability ever to possess what she is possessed by. (The difference between Emma, who sees every relation as "first," as new and original, and Charles, Rodolphe, Léon, and Lheureux, for whom she is never the first, establishes a binary opposition, Emma/men. Charles, however, resembles not only the three other men, but also Emma herself: though he has been married, he is still "virgin" ["It was he who might rather have been taken for the virgin of the evening before"], and his relation to Emma is, like her relation to the other men, so exclusive that her death means his own death. Thus, Charles's position is essentially double and ambiguous. I discuss this topic in greater detail in the next part of the [essay].) But unlike Marie of *Novembre*, Emma cannot recognize this repetition: she is "not in the least conscious of her prostitution." Thus, though Emma's story is similar to Marie's (both tell of the impossibility of satisfying desire) and also to Helen's in the *Tentation* (both tell of a growing sensuality, of a gradual "incarnation"), Emma remains only half aware of her "story" and, unlike the other two, cannot narrate it herself.

Every character in Flaubert is potentially a narrator. But Emma's imaginary existence (her narcissism) prevents her from fully realizing this potential. In the same way that the narrators (of the *Mémoires, Novembre,* the *Tentation*) create characters by doubling, by externalizing a part of themselves, magically evoking the other, so does Emma:

> But while writing to him, it was another man she saw, a phantom fashioned out of her most ardent memories, of her favorite books, her strongest desires, and at last he became so real, so tangible, that her heart beat wildly in awe and admiration,

though unable to see him distinctly, for, like God, he was hidden beneath the abundance of his attributes. He dwelt in that
azure land where silken ladders swung from balconies in the
moonlight, beneath a flower-scented breeze. She felt him near
her; he was coming and would ravish her entire being in a kiss.

Emma creates by doubling herself, by projecting images, spectacles.
But she can never go very far in giving these images life and specificity.
Even in this passage, which marks the greatest concretization she ever
achieves ("he became so real, so tangible"), the image of the lover, the
idealized other ("another man"), remains vague and abstract. The description ("he dwelt in that azure land") reminds us of the description of Helen
before she became "real" ("I was the moonlight, I penetrated the foliage,
I rolled over the flowers, I illuminated with my face the azure ether of
summer nights"), before she became specified in time and place, with a
body, with a history. The images Emma conjures up do not "come to
life" because she cannot let them become concrete, specific, that is, different from and independent of her. Emma dreams not too much but too
little—too little not in terms of the practical welfare of a provincial woman
but in terms of the possibility of creating fiction, of coming into being as
a narrator.

Emma does not understand why her dreams never come true ("Why
was her life so unsatisfactory," she asks herself). She tends to blame her
unhappiness on "fate" ("If fate had willed it"), her bad luck, her particular
situation in time and space—her reality. But we already know that in Flaubert "reality" is whatever has been externalized and differentiated enough
to become totally different from the self that gave rise to it. That Emma's
dreams do not come to life is therefore the fault not of her reality but of
her dreaming. Her dreams could come to life if she let them take on some
life. But Emma always arrests her dreams before they become concrete
and specific, independent of and different from her, real. Emma's dreams,
in other words, do not have plots; the images she projects remain so amor-
phous, so lacking life and concreteness, that they cannot act at all and so,
of course, can neither fulfill her desires nor provide her with a story to
narrate. This becomes clear when we compare Emma's dreams with one
of the dreams of the narrator-hero in *Novembre*.

In *Novembre* the "I" narcissistically doubles itself for the sake of erotic
satisfaction: "I called to Love! My lips trembled and went out as if I had
scented the breath of some other mouth." But the hero does not stop here.
The "double" becomes more and more real, concrete, alive, independent,

so that when the hero goes back to the city, he "sees" women who "seemed to smile on me, to invite me to silken loves; ladies in wraps bent from their balconies to see me, saying: 'Love us! Love us!' " Finally, this generalized femininity becomes even more concrete and particularized when it is incarnated in the figure of Marie: "There was Woman everywhere. . . . When I came to the street at last, after I walked for a century, I thought I should choke. . . . I went forward, forward. . . . Finally I entered a room. . . . A woman was seated. . . . She was wearing a white dress." The dream comes true (and the price will have to be paid).

But Emma's dreams never became stories: "With Walter Scott, later on, she fell in love with historical events, dreamed of guardrooms, old oak chests and minstrels. She would have liked to live in some old manorhouse, like those long-waisted chatelaines who, in the shade of pointed arches, spent their days leaning on the stone, chin in hand, watching a white-plumed knight galloping on his black horse from the distant field." This dream, like very other "vision" in Flaubert, is "en abîme": Emma sees herself as a lady of the manor who sees a knight coming toward her. But what is curious about this dream (and characteristic of all Emma's dreams) is its complete immobility; it is a frozen tableau, wholly lacking in action. Emma sees herself, but not, basically, as different from herself. Though the lady lives in an "old manor-house" and wears gowns with "long-waisted" bodices, she shares Emma's predicament and "activity," and spends her day dreaming, looking, expecting someone to come to her, waiting for her dream lover to become real. This in itself is not entirely surprising or new; after all, Saint Antoine, lying passive next to his hut, saw himself lying in a boat. But the similarity in the positions of the two Antoines was complemented by the difference—the activity—of the next relay, where the Saint was seen walking in Alexandria, killing and destroying, conversing with the Emperor. In Emma's dream the lack of action and mobility, the lack of difference, characterizes all relays. The dream lover is seen coming toward the lady but never actually reaching her—he is frozen on his black horse, and no matter how fast he gallops, he never arrives; he never comes true.

In her narcissism, then, Emma can neither see herself as different from herself nor give life to something that is independent of and different from herself. When she looks at keepsakes, what she sees are not different "possible lives," but different settings ("behind the balustrade of a balcony," "in carriages, gliding through parks," etc.) for an activity that is always the same: dreaming, looking, desiring. In her dream of a honeymoon with a dream lover, the only activity she can imagine is that of going toward another place ("to fly to those lands with sonorous names"); and after one arrives (but where?) the only activity possible remains that of desiring: "One looks at the stars, making plans for the future." Even when, just before she is to go away with Rodolphe, this dream of a perfect honeymoon seems about to come true, the situation is no different: she dreams about going away, and when, in the dream, they do arrive, nothing actually happens: "They would row in gondolas, swing in hammocks, and their existence would be easy and free as their wide silk gowns, warm and star-spangled as the nights they would contemplate. However, in the immensity of this future that she conjured up, nothing specific stood out; the days, all magnificent, resembled each other like waves; and the vision swayed in the horizon, infinite, harmonized, azure, and bathed in sunshine." (As we can see in this passage, the complete narcissism of Emma's dreams is also conveyed by the "intradiegetic" similes used here, on which Jacques Neef has commented in his "La Figuration réaliste." To a certain extent, in this novel Flaubert shares Emma's need to limit the narration to a reiteration of the same, to suppress developments that are different and differentiated. This is seen most clearly in his reworking of the drafts, where all deviations, all metaphors that were not "intradiegetic," all beginnings of other *récits* [especially through metaphors], have been ruthlessly eliminated. Flaubert, however, does not just repeat Emma's activity. The relation between implied author, narrator, and character is developed in the next part of this [essay].) Emma can conceive of herself only as what she is: desiring, expecting, going toward something. If she never actually arrives, if her dreams and expectations never come true, it is because she always stops too short: "At the end of some indefinite distance there was always a confused spot, into which her dream died."

Emma's dream about Paris is a particularly striking example of her incapability of generating difference. The dream is divided into distinct pictures, each of which is slightly more animated than the previous one, so that we engage in the typical Flaubertian movement toward materialization and concretization. The world of the ambassadors is simply the world of reflections, with its "polished floors" and "drawing rooms lined with mirrors." The only activity is that of "moving" (going elsewhere?). It is a totally specular world in which nothing can happen to ruffle its surface and break the reflection (hence, it is also a world of mystery and dissimulation). In the world of the duchesses, the women's activity is limited to being pale and wearing English point on their petticoats, and though the men are slightly more active, their activity is marked by futility (they "don't get anywhere"): "The men, their talents hidden under a frivolous appearance, rode horses to death at pleasure, spent the summer season at Baden, and finally, on reaching their forties, married heiresses." The world of the "writers and actresses" is clearly more alive (one eats there!) though again its activity is rather close to home: "They were . . . full of ambitious ideals and fantastic frenzies." What comes next? We might expect something more active still, something that will finally become fully alive (will develop into a story, into a plot); but no: "As for the rest of the world, it was lost, with no particular place, and as if nonexistent." This is what always happens to Emma's dreams: they always expire—die into "a confused spot"—when they arrive at a place where an activity other than looking, going elsewhere, dreaming, contemplating, desiring (that is, other than repetition without difference) would allow them to reveal difference and independence, become real. This place where the dream has to expire, that "rest of the world" she cannot bear to make precise, is "all her immediate surroundings." The locus of difference is, paradoxically, not "elsewhere," not far away, but right next to her, within arm's reach. That which surrounds her is what is different from her, independent of her, not subject to her control (hence, antagonistic, hostile); this is "real'"—"real" being whatever escapes the control of narcissistic projection.

The reality that is totally independent of Emma is crystallized in the figure of Homais. Though Homais probably speaks more than any other character in the novel, we are very seldom presented with his inner thoughts and feelings, either through direct discourse or through narrative description. This is because Homais, as an incarnation of "reality," cannot be represented as an individual: he does not have an interiority; he is totally empty, desexualized; he is the incarnation of the *Dictionnaire des idées reçues*.

As a representation of reality, Homais is totally excluded by Emma. He is the only important character in the novel who does not play a role in her drama, who is entirely superfluous to the main line of the story: her love relations and her gradual entanglement in monetary difficulties. Even at the very end of the novel, when Emma tries to borrow money from Guillaumin and goes so far as attempting to seduce Binet, the possibility of establishing some relation with the pharmicist never occurs to her. Though they live as neighbors and meet very often, they appear to be totally unaware of each other. We never see Homais looking at Emma; we never see her through his eyes (as we do through the eyes of Charles, Léon, and Rodolphe). Occasionally, we hear his "opinion" of her: "You are prettier than ever. You'll make *quite an impression* [*vous allez* faire flores] in Rouen" (Flaubert's emphasis), or "She is a real lady! She would not be

out of place in a sous-préfecture!'", but these opinons are always impersonal pronouncements rather than revelations of his private thoughts.
About Emma's view of Homais we know even less: we never see him
through her eyes; we never hear her opinion of him or her feelings toward
him. We do know that Emma and Léon think of Madame Homais—because she exists as an object that can conceivably be desired (Léon thinks
of this possibility, though negatively). Homais, however, simply does not
exist as a subject or as an object of desire.

The independence and autonomy that Homais enjoys, as an incarnation of reality, explain his menacing power—"he was becoming dangerous"—and justify his role as the impersonal agent of Emma's death. Even
though he is not involved directly and actively in Emma's destruction (as
is Lheureux), the poison that kills her has to come from his pharmacy.

It is this menacing quality of reality that explains Emma's refusal to
think about or accept what is close to her, though this is the only way to
make her dreams come true. And indeed, Homais, as an incarnation of reality, is not only external to Emma's existence and a threat; he is also represented as the place where Emma's desires are fulfilled. Whereas she is
frustrated in her desire for a son, he is the father of two; whereas she falls
further and further into debt, he is economically successful. He is famous,
his name is known to all; he achieves the reputation that Emma would like
to have, and that she tries to achieve, vicariously and without success,
through Charles: "Why at least, was not her husband one of those silently
determined men who work at their books all night, and at last . . . at
sixty . . . wear a string of medals on their ill-fitting black coat? She would
have wished this name of Bovary, which was hers, to be illustrious, to see
it displayed at the booksellers', repeated in the newspapers, known to all
France."

Homais fulfills these desires: "He busied himself with great questions:
the social problem, the moral plight of the poorer classes, pisciculture,
rubber, railways, etc. . . . He by no means gave up his store. On the contrary, he kept well abreast of new discoveries"; "The crowds . . . threatened at times to smash the window of the pharmacy . . . so great was
Homais's reputation in the neighboring villages"; "He has just been given
the cross of the Legion of Honor."

Emma's failure and frustration are the result of her narcissism, of her
imaginary existence, which does not allow any real difference. The only
difference Emma can permit is that of scenery, of setting, so that although
she retains her sameness and holds the projected image in specular subordination to herself, she can still create the illusion of difference. Her preoccu-

pation with the smallest details of clothes and scenery, furniture or accessories, points to her desire to create an illusion of difference where actually only sameness and repetition exist. What characterizes her both as a "dreamer" (a potential, though abortive, narrator) and as a character is her belief that a change in decor is sufficient to create a difference in experience.

Emma's attempt to create a semblance of difference explains the necessity of her entanglement with Lheureux. In her drama of desire, the objects of "setting" that he helps her acquire function as fetishes, as metonymic substitutes for what has never existed. Like fetishes, they perform a double task: they try to hide an absence and, in doing so, declare it. This basic inner contradiction, of which Emma is not aware, is what prevents the illusion of difference from providing real satisfaction. And because her desire is never fulfilled, she continues to buy, gets deeper in debt, until Lheureux, like Rodolphe and Léon, deserts her, bringing about her ruin, her death.

The theme of financial ruin is present in the novel from the outset: Charles's father squanders his wife's dowry, Héloïse is ruined by the bankruptcy of her banker, the doctor whose position and house Charles takes in Yonville was ruined by his extravagant expenses, Tellier, the owner of the Café Français, is gradually ruined by Lheureux. In her monetary drama, as in her love story, Emma can only repeat. Just as she is born into a world of discourse that creates her as a desiring self, so is she born into a socioeconomical world of squandering and ruin which she cannot help imitating. Just as in her narcissistic world true difference is not allowed, and accessories serve to create a physical (and hence "real") semblance of difference, so in the socioeconomical world in which she finds herself, money is the imaginary way of creating a "real" (sensuous) difference, where actual change cannot be brought about.

This parallelism between the stories of love and of monetary entanglement articulates the inner contradictions of narcissism of which Emma is a victim: beginning as a mode of existence in which the self does not allow any loss of itself, narcissism ends up as a squandering that wastes the self away and annihilates it: "What happiness she had known at that time, what freedom, what hope! what a wealth of illusions! It was all gone now. She had lost them [*elle en avait depensé*] one by one, at every stage in the growth of her soul, in the succession of her conditions." This inner contradiction explains why Emma, who always wants to coincide with herself and to minimize any difference between herself and the mirror images she creates, also desires to mingle and get confused with the other to the point of complete annihilation. Thus, for example, during the ball at the chateau of Vaubyessard, "she would have wanted to know their lives, to penetrate into them, to blend with them [*s'y confondre*]" or, during the visit to the church, "she would have liked to be once more lost [*confondue*] in the long line of white veils." The desire to unite with the other, to mingle to the point of complete fusion, is the obverse of the desire not to permit any difference to emerge, to abolish the space of difference.

Emma's need to create a semblance of difference explains not only her financial ruin (the plot of the novel), but also the particular quality of her dreaming (her existence as a potential narrator). In this respect, Emma's attention to the smallest detail of setting turns her narcissistic dreaming into "realistic" description. This so-called romantic heroine actually resembles a realistic narrator for whom the smallest detail of decor is important because it creates the illusion of reality, what Barthes called "l'effet du réel." Emma's "vraisemblance" (or "reality") as a character and her "realism" as a would-be narrator both result from her narcissism. Her fixation on one image each time (on one possible life) and her refusal to recognize the otherness and repetition within her, are precisely what enable her to emerge as a self with a consistent character. The self can exist as a self only if it remains unaware of the imaginariness of its existence; the moment it becomes aware of its imaginary existence and sees its own lack of integrity and originality, it is annihilated as a self. Emma remains a self because she does not see the otherness in herself; for the same reason, she is unable to project or create "reality"—otherness that escapes narcissistic control. As a narrator, therefore, she must create an "illusion of reality" by employing the devices of realism—the attention to detail and setting.

Ever since Jakobson's influential study on aphasia as a linguistic problem, realistic prose has been equated with the preference for metonymy over metaphor. It would be more exact to say that in the kind of realism Emma practices, the main effort is to metaphorize the metonymical; a counter-movement—of metonymizing those metaphors—betrays the existence of a narrator who, as we shall see, manifests his distance from Emma in various other ways, too.

Emma's metaphorizing can be seen in her attempt to transform signifiers into signifieds. In Emma's universe, objects and accessories, whole scenes, clothes, physical traits, all function as signifiers: "persecuted ladies fainting in lonely pavillions, . . . somber forests, heartaches, vows, sobs, tears and kisses, little boat rides by moonlight, nightingales in shady groves"—all these are signifiers whose signifieds are "bliss," "passion," "ecstasy," that is to say, other signifiers. Emma attempts to present these signifiers (bliss, passion, ecstasy) as signifieds. The "exotic elsewhere"

(Paris or Italy) is also a signifier (Paris, "a boundless name") that Emma transforms into a signified, in order to guarantee the truth and reality of the chain of signifiers—that is, give to this chain an appearance of non-arbitrariness. This readiness to see a signifier as a signified, the arbitrary as necessary, is dramatized in the plot when Léon makes Emma accept the ride in the carriage by explaining that "everybody does it in Paris."

Emma's entire relation to the world of signifiers into which literature introduces her, her great stake in dreaming up different setting for her plots, her relation to the world of objects around her, can all be summarized as an attempt to represent the arbitrariness of metonymic substitution as necessary and organic, that is, as metaphoric. But this attempt is handled ironically, showing that metaphor is in fact metonymy: "Did not love, like Indian plants, need a special soil, a special temperature? Sighs by moonlight, long embraces, tears flowing over yielded hands, all the passions of the flesh and the languors of tenderness seemed to her inseparable from the balconies of great castles where life flows idly by, from boudoirs with silken curtains and thick carpets, well-filled flowerstands, a bed on a raised dais, and from the flashing of precious stones and the golden braids of liveries."

The passage (in free indirect discourse) tries, on the other hand, to metaphorize the metonymic, to present the relation of contiguity as necessary. This is done through a metaphor: in the same way that plants need a special soil, love needs a certain setting. The relation between "love" and "setting" is therefore not arbitrary but necessary. But actually what one finds on the side of "love" is just as much of a setting as the "setting": "moonlight," "sighs," "tears." So within this metaphorization of the metonymy, one finds a metonymization of metaphor. In other words, the comparison attempts to show that the relationship between the signified "love" and its signifiers is not arbitrary. What the comparison actually betrays, however, is that "love" is itself just a signifier, and the relation between it and the other signifiers is therefore only a relation of contiguity and substitution.

The double movement of this passage, as well as the ambiguity of its free indirect discourse, indicate that Emma's narcissism does not account for the entire text: the text of *Madame Bovary* includes more than Madame Bovary. Let us now proceed to analyze the larger context in which Emma's existence is embedded.

The character of Emma marks a certain return to the narcissistic stance of the early works, where the subject enters into a dual and exclusive relationship with one image. This dual relationship causes the subject's death and annihilation—Emma dies repeatedly in the novel—and as a result, the narration cannot continue except by starting afresh with a new dual relationship. But in spite of this similarity with the early works, *Madame Bovary* is not really the same as *Les Mémoires d'un fou* or *Novembre*. *Madame Bovary* has a particular character as a novel because it combines an awareness of the necessity and inevitability of projecting multiplicity with the desire (on Emma's part) to transform this multiplicity back into unity. Emma refuses to view mulitiplicity as a succession (where one's attention continuously shifts from image to image, where substitution is unending, where there is no first or last), and attempts, instead, to view multiplicity as a totality, to encompass it in a single admiring, fascinated gaze. What results from this combining of multiplicity with simultaneity is a parceling out, a fragmentation, of the spectacle. For example, in the scene of the ball at the chateau of Vaubyessard, we read, "Along the line of seated women painted fans were fluttering, bouquets half-hid smiling faces [*le sourire des visages*], and gold-stoppered scent-bottles were turned in half-clenched hands, with white gloves outlining the nail and tightening on the flesh at the wrists. Lace trimmings, diamond brooches, medallion brackets trembled on blouses, gleamed on breasts, clinked on bare arms." There are no distinct, complete, unified figures because the scene, on the one hand, offers a multiplicity of images while Emma, on the other, refuses to view this multiplicity as a sequence (in the way Jules or Saint Antoine had done). Rather, she tries to encompass the multiplicity in one gaze, transform it into one image that will give her back her own reflection as a unified, idealized figure.

Emma's story itself is structured as a sequence in which one object of desire is substituted for another. Her story has a succession, but it is a succession that Emma refuses to be fully conscious of. And since she deliberately tries to ignore the very existence of the sequence, its order cannot depend on her. Hence there is no attempt in the text to represent her successive encounters (with Charles, the Viscount, Léon, etc.) as responses to an internal, psychological necessity. Rather, they are represented as totally fortuitous, the result of pure chance. However, when we look a bit more closely at this "chance," we see that a better name for it is "Charles." It is Charles who is invited to the ball at Vaubyessard where Emma meets the Viscount; it is Charles whom Rodolphe is seeking when he first catches sight of Emma, and it is Charles who encourages her to go riding with Rodolphe; it is Charles who meets Léon at the Opera in Rouen where Emma is present at Charles's insistence. "Fate" in the novel is not

Rodolphe ("Roldophe who had been the agent of this fate") but Charles—
and like fate, he is blind to the consequences and meaning of his acts. He
never suspects what he does. And yet he is not totally passive (as Emma
is, chosen and deserted by the men Charles throws in her way); he is in
fact the active force that keeps the novel going. He is the blind orchestra-
tor of the series, of the sequence of events that constitutes, both *Madame
Bovary* and the life and death of Emma.

Charles's place and role in the novel have been much discussed. The
problem he presents is both structural (why does the novel start and end
with him) and psychological (why does he no longer have an inner life in
the middle part of the novel). The structural and the psychological are related, however, and the combined "problem" can be explained by the basic structure of the Flaubertian text, which requires a character-narrator to
retreat to the margin of the text and "die" so that the spectacle he has projected can come to life.

The Charles of the beginning of the novel (before meeting Emma) is
a rather typical Flaubertian hero, both in his capacity to dream and in his
"stupidity," his inability to understand words and objects (he is thus similar in one respect to Jules and in another to Henry of the first *Education*).
His marriage does not fulfill his expectations and his disillusionment is followed by the night visit to the Bertaux. This visit, with its long, detailed
description (totally irrelevant in terms of plot), emerges as the classical
scene in which the Flaubertian hero, amidst the typical landscape and totally enclosed within himself, doubles himself and is about to create a
story:

> Still sleepy from the warmth of his bed, he let himself be lulled
> by the quiet trot of his horse. . . . The flat country stretched as
> far as eye could see, and the tufts of trees around the farms
> seemed, at long intervals, like dark violet stains on the vast
> grey surface, fading on the horizon into the gloom of the sky.
> Charles from time to time opened his eyes but his mind grew
> weary, and sleep coming upon him, he soon fell into a doze
> wherein his recent sensations blending with memories, he be-
> came conscious of a double self, at once student and married
> man, lying in his bed as but now, and crossing the operation
> theater as of old. The warm smell of poultices mingled in his
> brain with the fresh odour of dew; he heard the iron rings rat-
> tling along the curtain-rods of the bed and saw his wife
> sleeping.

This scene of doubling and creation is followed by the appearance of Emma, who gradually dominates the narrative, so that it is no longer Charles's story but hers. This should remind us of the movement of the narration in *Novembre,* where the doubling of the narrator is followed by his meeting with Marie, which results in the transformation of the narration from the story of the narrator's life into the story of Marie's life.

Charles's career, then, is the common one in Flaubert: it repeats the move from what I have called the interests of the character (narcissistic doubling) to the interests of the narrator (death of the self, which permits the story to unfold). That some of the characters (Charles, Léon) turn into satisfied bourgeois is a representational necessity, as is the growing sensuality (materialization, incarnation) of other characters, like Emma. Charles's lack of psychological depth and "personality," his stupidity, results from his having retired to the margin of the novel where, blind and empty, unconscious, he can push the plot forward by arranging opportunities for Emma to have love affairs, can give life to his surrogate character and create a story.

But Charles is not present at the very beginning of the narration, and he himself is seen (created, projected) by a narrator who soon after creating him, disappears, dies as consciousness or memory: "It would be impossible for any one of us to remember anything about him." The relationship between the narrator who says "we" and "Charles" is far from simple. Though it is the "we" that opens the narration with the act of "seeing" Charles ("We were in class when the headmaster came in, followed by a *new boy*" Flaubert's emphasis), this "we" is not simply a rhetorical amplification of the creating-I (eye), a repetition of the "I" of the *Mémoires* or *Novembre.* For, as Thibaudet has shrewdly observed, it is also *Charles* who repeats the "I" of the earlier works: he is the outsider, mocked by others (*Mémoires:* "I lived there lonely and bored, bothered by my masters and mocked by my companions"). But whereas the *Mémoires* presents the existence of a hostile, antagonistic world from the point of view of the "I" who suffers because of his superiority ("They, laugh at me! they, so weak, so common, with such limited minds; me, whose mind was inundated at the limits of creation [*moi, dont l'esprit se noyait sur les limites de la création*]"), at the opening of *Madame Bovary* the antagonism between the "I" and the hostile world is presented from the outside, from the point of view of a world that sees the difference of the "I" as ridiculous.

Thus in the relation between the "we" and "Charles," the "I" can be located in either or both. We cannot determine which comes first, whether the creative-I is "Charles," the dreamer who presents the outside world as hostile and antagonistic (in a scenario similar to that of the *Mémoires*), or whether it is the "we," presenting the other that is differentiated from it as different—hence stupid and ridiculous.

The relation of the "I" to "Charles" and the "we" is therefore analogous to the relation of the narrator to Jules and Henry in the first *Education sentimentale:* in the first *Education* the narrator, instead of creating a character that will be his mirror image, saw himself as divided into two different forces-characters; in *Madame Bovary* the creating-I (whom we can call, using Booth's term, the implied author) is split between "we" and "Charles." But whereas in *L'Education sentimentale* the two different points of view are clear and distinct and we simply alternate between them, in *Madame Bovary* we have both points of view simultaneously and cannot always tell which is which.

The indeterminacy of narrative perspective in *Madame Bovary* is complemented by an indeterminancy of narrative voice, created by the dominance, in this novel, of free indirect discourse. Free indirect discourse is an utterance whose speaker cannot be determined: the speaker may be the narrator, or one of the characters, or both, or neither. The chapter in which Emma's education is described, for example, starts with a straightforward narration: "She had read *Paul et Virginie,* and she had dreamed of the little bamboo-house." The point of view of the narrator who describes Emma is clearly distinct from the "vision" (dream) of Emma; we know we have a narrator who talks about a character from whom he is distinct. But a few lines later the balance starts to shift, and instead of a narrator who takes a distance from the character he talks about, we see the narrator merging with the character: "But above all [she had dreamed] of the sweet friendship of some dear little brother, who seeks red fruit for you." The appearance of "you" situates both narrator and reader within the narration and thus abolishes the distance between narrator and character. However, in this phrase, the vision (the dream) is still clearly attributed to Emma. Not so in the following phrase, with the direct evocation "And you, too, were there, Sultans with long pipes," where it seems as if it is the narrator who sees the Sultans, rather than (or together with) Emma. A few lines later the distinction between narrator and character disappears completely: "Emma was secretly pleased that she had reached at a first attempt the rare ideal of delicate lives [*existences pâles*], never attained by mediocre hearts." We can no longer tell whether the narrator, in talking about "the rare ideal of delicate lives," is quoting Emma (reporting her words, or her feelings, or her thoughts) or speaking in his own voice (or expressing his own opinions and feelings). This merging of voices—which we call free indirect discourse—blurs the distinction between different points of view, different projections; it is the mode of narration that accounts for large portions of the novel (the chapter that follows the one from which I have just quoted—part 1, chapter 7—is written almost entirely in free indirect discourse).

The fusion of the narrative voice and the voice of a character in free indirect discourse is possible only because, on another level, the narrator and the character are clearly distinguished (for example, the narration is not in the first person). Free indirect discourse, therefore, stabilizes and freezes, so to speak, the alternation between different points of view—hence the enormous difference between a work like *Novembre* or even the first *Education,* and a work like *Madame Bovary,* though all three, as I have shown, have the same basic structure. In the early works the constant oscillation between clearly differentiated points of view created a rhythm of mystification and demystification, but in *Madame Bovary,* where free indirect discourse accounts for a large portion of the text, this alternation is impossible. We have a thing and its opposite at the same time, always.

In the following pages I will be speaking about problems of narration that are usually discussed under the heading of either "narrative voice" or "point of view." I find Uspenski's distinction among points of view on the spatio-temporal, ideological, psychological, and phraseological planes more accurate, inasmuch as it allows us to differentiate not only between "who sees" and "who speaks," but also between "who feels" and "who thinks." Such distinctions are needed because we cannot *a priori* assume that these planes coincide. In my discussion of Flaubert up to now I have emphasized the importance of the act of seeing—projecting images, creating a spectacle—as constitutive of the act of narration; voice seems to be secondary, added to make the vision accessible to an audience (the reader, another character). However, our discussion of the complex relation between language and experience has already suggested that such a separation is oversimplified: what one "sees" is always to some extent shaped by language, by what one (or someone) says. Although there is great methodological merit in keeping questions of vision, voice, knowledge, distance, and the like separate from one another, we should also realize that in Flaubert's texts such distinctions are not always possible. More specifically, in *Madame Bovary* narrators can differ from each other in one respect and yet be indistinguishable in another respect, so that we cannot identify a distinct "voice" or a distinct "vision." What characterizes *Madame Bovary* is not simply the existence of different narrators, but our inability to pinpoint portions of the text as originating with a specific narrator. We do not alternate between different narrators but are always in the presence of a narration that according to one criterion (vision, voice, omniscience, distance, and so on) belongs to one narrator, but according to a different criterion belongs to another. The source of the narration is undecidable, and instead of having multiple narrators (each of which can still have a distinct identity), we have an "exploded" narrator who does not have a distinct set of characteristics and cannot therefore be opposed to another narrator, or to a character.

As we have seen, the novel starts with an ambiguous narrator: "we" who sees Charles or Charles who sees "the world." But this complex subjective narrator is also complemented by an omniscient narrator who narrates the detailed story of the life of Charles Bovary and who identifies himself as different from the "we"—as not belonging to the community of students: "There was a burst of laughter from the boys which . . . thoroughly put the poor lad out of countenance"; "Quiet was restored. Heads bent over desks." The scene is narrated alternately from two contradictory points of view (subjective and objective, internal and external), so that even if we can determine the source of specific details, the scene as a whole cannot be attributed to a single narrator. The same technique is employed in other places—for example, in the wedding chapter (part 1, chap. 4).

The two different narrators (omniscient and non-omniscient, external and internal) cannot, however, be clearly distinguished in the way they see—that is, cannot be clearly distinguished *qua* narrators. Examples of this similarity in vision between otherwise different points of view are the descriptions of Charles and Héloïse in the first part of the novel.

The description of Charles seems to be presented by the narrator "we"; it starts with a reference to "the *new boy* [who] was . . . taller than any one of us" (Flaubert's emphasis). The description of Charles's first wife is presented by the other narrator, the one who knows all the details of Charles's life, from before his birth to the present moment, and who survives the "we." Both these descriptions, however, follow precisely the same method: they move from top to bottom, attempting to give a total, unified picture. Thus, the description of Charles:

> His *hair* was cut square on his *forehead* like a village choir boy;
> he looked reliable, but very ill at ease. Although he was not
> *broad-shouldered,* his short jacket of green cloth with black buttons must have been tight about the *armholes,* and showed at
> the opening of the cuffs red *wrists* accustomed to being bare.

> His *legs,* in blue stockings, looked out from beneath yellowish trousers, drawn tight by suspenders. He wore stout, ill-cleaned, hob-nailed *boots.* (my italics)

Similarly, the description of Héloïse:

> She had long *teeth;* wore in all weathers a little black shawl, the edge of which hung down between her *shoulder-blades;* her bony figure was sheathed in her clothes as if they were a scabbard; they were too short, and displayed her *ankles* with the laces of her large *boots* crossed over grey stockings. (my italics)

This method of description differs totally from others used in the novel—for example, the impressionistic portrayal of the main residents of Yonville, who are described (presumably by the omniscient narrator) with two or three revelatory details, mainly of clothing. Homais, for instance, is "a man in green leather slippers, slightly pockmarked, and wearing a velvet cap with a gold tassel."

Things are even more complicated because the description of Héloïse may equally well be attributed to Charles, since the passage in question is in free indirect discourse. The description is preceded by Charles's thoughts and feelings, after which comes the phrase "and then the widow was thin; she had . . . ," which makes it possible for us to interpret the whole description as expressing Charles's point of view. In the rest of the novel, however, Charles has a very different way of perceiving. He never attempts to unify details into a total picture but retains a fragmented view, as can be seen in his associative, fragmentary perception of Emma: "Her nails were shiny, delicate at the tips, more polished than the ivory of Dieppe, and almond-shaped. Yet her hand was not beautiful, perhaps not white enough, and a little hard at the knuckles. . . . Her real beauty was in her eyes. Although brown they seemed black because of the lashes."

In fiction, the way characters are named is usually a clear indication of narrative voice (or of point of view on the phraseological plane). In *Madame Bovary,* however, the way characters are named may change from sentence to sentence, indicating such a shifting point of view that no single narrator could be the source of the passage as a whole. For example, in a short paragraph dealing with the insufficiency of Charles's education at the hands of the village priest, the subjective point of view ("Charles could not go on like this" and references to Charles as "the child [*le gamin*]") is contrasted with an external point of view (Charles's parents are called "Madame" and "Monsieur") to produce the following: "Charles could not go on like this. Madame took strong steps. Ashamed, or rather tired out, Monsieur gave in without a struggle, and they waited one year longer, so that the child could take his first communion." Similarly, concerning the lessons given Charles by the priest, we read:

> Or else the *curé,* if he had not to got out, sent for *his pupil* after the Angelus. *They [on]* went up to his room and settled down; the flies and moths fluttered round the candle. It was close, *the child* fell asleep, and *the good man,* beginning to doze with his hands on his stomach, was soon snoring with his mouth wide open. On other occasions, when *Monsieur le Curé,* on his way back after administering the holy oil to some sick person in the neighborhood, caught sight of *Charles* playing about the fields, he called him, lectured him for a quarter of an hour, and took advantage of the occasion to make him conjugate his verb at the foot of a tree. (my italics)

Not only does the way of naming change, preventing us from pinpointing the narrative voice, but it also bears an arbitrary relation to our acquaintance with the characters' thoughts and feelings. What we called point of view on the phraseological plane is sometimes in conflict with point of view on the psychological plane. An example of such conflict appears in the first part of the novel, where the reader sees Emma through Charles's eyes and is given direct access to his thoughts; yet the way Charles is named in those passages suggests an external, distant narrator. One such description ends as follows: "And just showing the tip of the ear [her hair] was joined behind in a thick chignon, with a wavy movement at the temples that the *country doctor* saw now for the first time in his life" (my italics).

The point of view in *Madame Bovary* changes so rapidly that it is impossible to attribute a chapter, a paragraph, and sometimes even a sentence to one narrator. In addition, the phraseological, psychological, ideological, and spatio-temporal planes do not coincide, so that even if we can determine who feels, thinks, or sees a certain detail, we cannot conclude with certainty who speaks. Whereas Emma is the narcissistic creator who opts for preserving an (imaginary) self at the price of aborted narration and perpetual death, the entire novel in which she is but one character is made possible by a succession, or even an indeterminacy, of points of view. By combining these two modes of creation, *Madame Bovary* can become a fully developed narrative and at the same time be centered on a self with a stable (even if only imaginary) identity.

We have seen that Emma is represented as a narcissistic character who refuses to see the repetition in her life, the lack of originality of her desire, the imaginary nature of her existence. This mode of representation creates an ironic juxtaposition of levels whereby the text says—lets the reader understand—what Emma herself is not aware of. In other words, the larger context in which Emma's existence is embedded can be seen as demystifying her narcissistic attitude. But at the same time the indeterminacy of point of view fragments the narrator to such an extent that he cannot be seen as a coherent entity, distinct from the characters; through the use of free indirect discourse, the voice of the narrator and that of the narrated character merge. Thus the novel must be read on two levels simultaneously. On one level, Emma's narcissistic attitude is treated ironically, but on another level this demystifying activity is in itself undermined: the narrator cannot be seen as more authoritative and insightful than the character whose mystification and error he exposes because he himself cannot be clearly distinguished from that character. The separation between narrator and character necessary for sustaining the authority of an ironic discourse is undermined. In *Madame Bovary* the implied author both takes an ironic distance from his character and shows the impossibility of this ironic distance. The relation between narrator and character in *Madame Bovary* is characterized by neither (or by both) identification nor (and) clear separation and difference.

Chronology

1821	December 13, Gustave Flaubert is born to Achille-Chéophas, a surgeon, and Caroline Fleuriot.
1834	At the lycée, Flaubert edits the journal *Art et progrès* and begins to write fiction.
1836	Writes a number of stories and novellas. Falls passionately in love with a woman much his senior, Madame Schlésinger, and begins to write *Mémoires d'un fou*.
1837–39	Continues to write many short stories and novellas, including *Smarh,* as well as some nonfiction works.
1840	Flaubert receives his Baccalaureate and then travels through the Pyrenées and Corsica.
1842	Moves to Paris to study law, meets Maxime Du Camp, and writes *Novembre*.
1843	Meets Victor Hugo, sees the Schlésingers often, and begins the first *Education sentimentale*.
1844	Has his first attack, probably epileptic, at Pont l'Evêque. Abandons studies and lives at home as a semi-invalid. The Flaubert family buys Croisset, the estate where Gustave will spend the rest of his life. He devotes himself completely to literature.
1845	Travels with his sister Caroline and her husband on their honeymoon to Italy. There, Gustave sees the painting by Brueghel which will inspire *La Tentation de saint Antoine*. Finishes the first *Education sentimentale*.
1846	On January 15 Achille-Cléophas dies, seven days before the birth of Caroline's daughter Caroline. A month later, the elder Caroline dies. Gustave begins *La Tentation de saint Antoine*. In June, he meets Louise Colet, a poet living in Paris. They become lovers in July.

1847   Beginning on May 1, Flaubert and Du Camp take a three month walking trip through Brittany and Normandy. Upon their return, Flaubert writes the odd and Du Camp the even chapters of *Par les champs et par les grèves,* published after Flaubert's death.

1848   February 23, Flaubert goes to Paris with Bouilhet to see the demonstrations, and briefly, joins them.

1849   Finishes *La Tentation* on September 12 and reads it, for three days, to Du Camp and Bouilhet. They declare it "unpublishable." Flaubert and Du Camp depart for a voyage to the Orient. They leave Marseilles on November 4 and go to Malta, Alexandria, and Cairo, where they remain until February of the following year.

1850   The voyage continues up the Nile, to Thebes, the Red Sea, Beirut, the Holy Land, Rhodes, Constantinople, and Athens.

1851   Flaubert and Du Camp travel through Sparta, Thermopylae, Patras, Naples, and Rome, where they are met by Flaubert's mother. Flaubert continues on to Florence, Venice, Cologne, and Brussels, and returns to Croisset in June. In July, he resumes his affair with Louise Colet, and later begins *Madame Bovary*.

1852–55   Works intensively on *Madame Bovary*. The relationship with Louise Colet ends in 1854, communication with her ends the following year.

1856   *Madame Bovary* is completed and appears in six somewhat censored installments in *La Revue de Paris* between October 1 and December 15. Fragments of the second *Tentation* are published in the *Artiste*.

1857   Trial and acquittal of *Madame Bovary*. Flaubert is made famous and the novel appears in book form. Flaubert begins to work on *Salammbô*.

1858–62   Writes *Salammbô*, which is published on November 4, 1862.

1863   A year of great social activity. Flaubert is often at Princess Mathilda's salon, he meets Turgenev at the Maghy dinners, visits Taine, and begins his correspondence with George Sand.

1864–69   Writes and publishes *L'Education sentimentale*.

1870   Flaubert is ill and works on *La Tentation*. The Franco-Prussian War breaks out, Prussian troops are quartered at Croisset, and Flaubert and his mother take refuge in Rouen.

1871–72   Completes *La Tentation de saint Antoine*.

1873   Friendship with Guy de Maupassant. Later in the year, writes *Le Candidat,* a four-act comedy.

1874   Production and failure of *Le Candidat* and publication of *La Tentation*. Flaubert travels to Switzerland and Normandy to do research for *Bouvard et Pécuchet*.

1875   Works on *Bouvard et Pécuchet,* but later, due to poor health and finances, temporarily abandons it to work on *La Légende de saint Julien l'Hospitalier*.

1876–77   Completes *Saint Julien, Un Coeur simple,* and *Hérodias*. The three pieces are published as *Trois Contes*. Flaubert returns to his work on *Bouvard et Pécuchet*.

1878–79   Continues to work on *Bouvard et Pécuchet*. In June 1879, the government grants Flaubert a commission of 3000 francs a year.

1880   Begins the last chapter of *Bouvard et Pécuchet*. On May 8, as he is working, Flaubert dies suddenly, perhaps of a cerebral hemorrhage.

1881   Posthumous publication of *Bouvard et Pécuchet*.

1884   Publication of Flaubert's letters to George Sand.

Contributors

HAROLD BLOOM, Sterling Professor of the Humanities at Yale University, is the author of *The Anxiety of Influence, Poetry and Repression,* and many other volumes of literary criticism. His forthcoming study, *Freud: Transference and Authority,* attempts a full-scale reading of all of Freud's major writings. A MacArthur Prize Fellow, he is general editor of five series of literary criticism published by Chelsea House. During 1987–88, he served as Charles Eliot Norton Professor of Poetry at Harvard University.

VICTOR BROMBERT is Henry Putnam University Professor of Romance Languages at Princeton University. His works include *The Romantic Prison, The Novels of Flaubert,* and *Victor Hugo and the Visionary Novel.*

LEO BERSANI is the Chairman of the French Department at the University of California, Berkeley. His books include *Balzac to Beckett: Center and Circumference in French Literature, A Future for Astyanax: Character and Desire in Literature, The Death of Stéphane Mallarmé,* and *The Freudian Body.*

TONY TANNER is a Fellow of King's College, Cambridge. His books include *The Reign of Wonder: Naivety and Reality in American Literature, City of Words: American Fiction 1950–1970,* and *Adultery in the Novel: Contrast and Transgression.* He has also written on Charlotte Brontë, Jane Austen, Henry James, Joseph Conrad, Saul Bellow, and Thomas Pynchon.

NAOMI SCHOR is Professor of French Studies at Brown University. She is the author of *Zola's Crowds* and *Breaking the Chains: Women, Theory, and French Realist Fiction,* and an editor of *Flaubert and Postmodernism.*

HAZEL BARNES teaches in the Department of the Comparative Literature at the University of Colorado, Boulder. She is the author of *An Existentialist Ethics, Humanistic Existentialism: The Literature of Possibility,* and *Sartre and Flaubert.*

DOMINICK LACAPRA is Professor of Intellectual History at Cornell University. His works include *Emile Durkheim: Sociologist and Philosopher*, *Madame Bovary on Trial*, and *Rethinking Intellectual History*.

MICHAL PELED GINSBURG is Professor of Comparative Literature and Chairman of the Department of French and Italian at Northwestern University. She is the author of *Flaubert Writing: A Study in Narrative Strategies*.

Bibliography

Ahearn, Edward J. "Using Marx to Read Flaubert: The Case of *Madame Bovary*."
In *L'Hénaurme Siècle. A Miscellany of Essays on Nineteenth-Century French Litera-ture,* edited by Will L. McLendon. Heidelberg: Carl Winter, 1984.

Bardèche, Maurice. *L'Oeuvre de Flaubert.* Paris: Les sept couleurs, 1974.

Bart, Benjamin F. *Flaubert.* Syracuse: State University of New York, 1967.

———, ed. Madame Bovary *and the Critics: A Collection of Essays.* New York: New York University Press, 1966.

Barthes, Roland. "L'Effet du réel." *Communications* 11 (1968): 84–89.

———. "Flaubert et la phrase." *Word* 24 (1968): 48–54.

Baudelaire, Charles. "*Madame Bovary* par Gustave Flaubert." In *Baudelaire as a Lit-erary Critic,* edited and translated by Lois B. Hyslop and Francis E. Hyslop, 138–49. University Park: Pennsylvania State University Press, 1964.

Berg, William J., Michel Grimaud, and George Moskos, eds. *Saint/Oedipus: Psy-chocritical Approaches to Flaubert's Art.* Ithaca: Cornell University Press, 1982.

Bersani, Leo. "The Narrator and the Bourgeois Community in *Madame Bovary*." *The French Review* 32 (1958): 527–33.

Bloom, Harold, ed. *Modern Critical Views: Gustave Flaubert.* New Haven: Chelsea House, 1987.

Bonnefis, Philippe. "Récit et histoire dans *Madame Bovary*." In *Linguistique et lit-térature,* Colloque de Cluny (1968): 157–63. "La Nouvelle Critique" special issue.

Bopp, Léon. *Commentaire sur* Madame Bovary. Neuchâtel: La Baconière, 1951.

Brombert, Victor. *Flaubert par lui-même.* Paris: Seuil, 1971.

———. *The Novels of Flaubert.* Princeton: Princeton University Press, 1966.

Brown, James W. "Aesthetic and Ideological Coalescence in the Alimentary Sign: *Madame Bovary*." In *Fictional Meals and Their Function in the French Novel: 1749–1848,* 131–70. Toronto: University of Toronto Press, 1984.

Buck, Stratton. *Gustave Flaubert.* New York: Twayne, 1966.

Carlut, Charles, ed. *Essais sur Flaubert en l'honneur du professeur Don Demorest.* Paris: Nizet, 1979.

Cascardi, Anthony J. "The Female Quixote: Aesthetics and Seduction." *The Bounds of Reason: Cervantes, Dostoevsky, Flaubert.* New York: Columbia University Press, 1986.

Conroy, Mark. *Modernism and Authority: Strategies of Legitimation in Flaubert and Conrad.* Baltimore: Johns Hopkins University Press, 1985.

Crouzet, Michel. "Le Style épique dans *Madame Bovary.*" *Europe* 485–87 (September–November 1969): 151–72.

Culler, Jonathan. *Flaubert, The Uses of Uncertainty.* Ithaca: Cornell University Press, 1974.

———. "The Uses of *Madame Bovary.*" *Diacritics* 11, no. 3 (1981): 74–81.

Daniels, Graham. "Emma Bovary's Opera—Flaubert, Scott, and Donizetti." *French Studies* 32 (1978): 285–303.

Debray-Genette, Raymonde. *Flaubert.* Paris: Firmin-Didot Étude et librairie Marcel Didier, 1970.

———, ed. *Flaubert à l'oeuvre.* Paris: Flammarion, 1980.

Demorest, D. L. *L'Expression figurée et symbolique dans l'oeuvre de Gustave Flaubert.* Paris: Les Presses Modernes, 1931.

Derrida, Jacques. "An Idea of Flaubert: 'Plato's letter.' " *MLN* 99 (1984): 748–68.

Diamond, Marie J. *The Problem of Aesthetic Discontinuity.* Port Washington, N.Y.: Kennikat Press, 1975.

Donato, Eugenio. "Flaubert and the Question of History: Notes for a Critical Anthology." *MLN* 91 (1976): 850–70.

Durry, Marie-Jeanne. *Flaubert et ses projets inédits.* Paris: Nizet, 1950.

Engstrom, Alfred G. "Flaubert's Correspondence and the Ironic and Symbolic Structure of *Madame Bovary.*" *Studies in Philology* 46 (1946): 470–95.

Europe 485–87 (September–November 1969). Special Flaubert issue.

Felman, Shoshana. "Gustave Flaubert: Living Writing, or Madness as Cliché." In *Writing and Madness,* translated by Martha Noel Evans, Brian Massumi, and Shoshana Felman. Ithaca: Cornell University Press, 1985.

Flaubert, Gustave. *Gustave Flaubert's* Madame Bovary. A Norton Critical Edition. Edited and translated by Paul de Man. New York: Norton, 1965.

Gaillard, Françoise. "Quelques notes pour une lecture idéologique de *Madame Bovary.*" *Revue des Sciences Humaines* 151 (1973): 463–68.

Genette, Gérard. "Flaubert par Proust." *L'Arc* 79 (1979): 3–17.

———. "Flaubert's Silences." In *Figures of Literary Discourse,* translated by Alan Sheridan. New York: Columbia University Press, 1982.

Gerhardi, Gerhard. "Romantic Love and the Prostitution of Politics." *Studies in the Novel* 4 (1972): 402–15.

Giraud, Raymond, ed. *Flaubert: A Collection of Critical Essays.* Englewood Cliffs, N.J.: Prentice-Hall, 1964.

Goodwin, Sarah Webster. "Emma Bovary's Dance of Death." *Novel* 19 (1985): 197–215.

Gothot-Mersch, Claudine. *La Genèse de* Madame Bovary. Paris: José Corti, 1966.

———. Introduction to *Madame Bovary.* Paris: Garnier, 1971.

———. "Le Point de vue dans *Madame Bovary.*" *Cahiers de l'Association Internationale des Études Françaises* 23 (1971): 243–59.

———, ed. *La Production du sens chez Flaubert.* Actes du Colloque de Cérisy. Paris: UGE, 1975.

Gray, Eugene F. "The Clinical View of Life: Gustave Flaubert's *Madame Bovary*

In *Medicine and Literature,* edited by Edmund Pellegrino. Peschel, N.Y.: N. Watson, 1980: 60–84.

Haig, Stirling. *Flaubert and the Gift of Speech.* New York: Cambridge University Press, 1986.

James, Henry. "Style and Morality in *Madame Bovary.*" In *Notes on Novelists with Some Other Notes.* New York: Scribner's, 1942: 59–66.

Jameson, Fredric. "Sartre in Search of Flaubert." *New York Times Book Review,* 27 December 1981.

Johnson, William A. "*Madame Bovary:* Romanticism, Modernism, and Bourgeois Style." *MLN* 94 (1979): 843–50.

Knight, Diana. *Flaubert's Characters: The Language of Illusion.* Cambridge: Cambridge University Press, 1985.

LaCapra, Dominick. Madame Bovary *on Trial.* Ithaca: Cornell University Press, 1982.

Lapp, John C. "Art and Hallucination in Flaubert." *French Studies* 10 (1956): 322–33.

Levin, Harry. *The Gates of Horn: A Study of the French Realists.* New York: Oxford University Press, 1963.

Lowe, Margaret. *Towards the Real Flaubert: A Study of* Madame Bovary. Oxford: Clarendon, 1984.

Lubbock, Percy. "The Craft of Fiction in *Madame Bovary.*" In *The Craft of Fiction,* 77–92. New York: Viking, 1957.

Lukacher, Maryline F. "Flaubert's Pharmacy." *Nineteenth-Century French Studies* 14 (1985–86): 37–50.

Lukàcs, Georg. *The Historical Novel.* Translated by Hannah and Stanley Mitchell. Middlesex: Penguin, 1969.

Masson, Bernard. "Le Corps d'Emma." In *Flaubert, la femme, la ville,* edited by Armand Lanoux. Paris: PUF, 1983.

Mathet, Marie-Thérèse. "Madame (Bovary)." *Poétique* 43 (1980): 346–53.

Mercié, Jean-Luc H. "*Madame Bovary:* Lecture d'un fragment de la noce." *Romanic Review* 71 (1980): 295–306.

Moreau, Pierre. "L'Art de la composition dans *Madame Bovary.*" *Orbis Litterarum* 12 (1957): 171–78.

Picard, Michel. "La Prodigalité d'Emma Bovary." *Littérature* 10 (1973): 77–97.

Pistorius, George. "La Structure des comparaisons dans *Madame Bovary.*" *Cahiers de l'Association Internationale des Études Françaises* 23 (1971): 223–42.

Pontalis, J.-B. "La Maladie de Flaubert." Parts 1, 2. *Les Temps modernes,* nos. 100, 101 (1954): 1646–59, 1889–1902.

Porter, Lawrence M., ed. *Critical Essays on Gustave Flaubert.* Boston: G. K. Hall, 1986.

Poulet, Georges. "The Circle and the Center: Reality and *Madame Bovary.*" *Western Review* 19 (1955): 245–60.

———. "Flaubert." In *The Metamorphoses of the Circle.* Baltimore: The Johns Hopkins University Press, 1966.

Prendergast, Christopher. "Flaubert: Writing and Negativity." *Novel* 9 (1975): 197–213.

Prince, Gerald. "On Attributive Discourse in *Madame Bovary*." In *Pretext, Text, Context,* edited by Robert L. Mitchell, 269–75. Columbus: Ohio State University Press, 1980.

Proust, Marcel. "À-propos du 'style' de Flaubert." *Nouvelle Revue Française* 14 (1920): 22–90.

Reinhart, Keith. "The Structure of *Madame Bovary*." *The French Review* 31 (1958): 300–306.

Richard, Jean-Pierre. "La création de la forme chez Flaubert." In *Littérature et sensation,* 119–219. Paris: Seuil, 1954.

Riffaterre, Michael. "Flaubert's Presuppositions." *Diacritics* 11, no. 4 (1981): 2–11.

Rothfield, Lawrence. "From Semiotic to Discursive Intertextuality: The Case of *Madame Bovary*." *Novel* 19 (1985): 57–80.

Rousset, Jean. "*Madame Bovary* ou le livre sur rien." In *Forme et signification: Essais sur les structures littéraires de Corneille à Claudel,* 109–33. Paris: José Corti, 1962.

Sabiston, Elisabeth J. *The Prison of Womanhood.* New York: St. Martin's Press, 1987.

Sainte-Beuve, Charles Augustin. "*Madame Bovary* par Gustave Flaubert." In *Causeries du lundi: Portraits littéraires et Portraits de femmes* 13, 4 May 1857, 283–97. Paris: Garnier, 1900.

Sartre, Jean-Paul. *The Family Idiot: Gustave Flaubert: 1821–1857,* vol. 1, translated by Carol Cosman. Chicago: University of Chicago Press, 1981.

———. *L'Idiot de la famille.* 3 vols. Paris: Gallimard, 1971/1972.

———. "Sartre's Notes for the Fourth Volume of *The Family Idiot*." Translated by Philippe Hunt and Philip Wood. *Yale French Studies* 68 (1985): 165–88.

———. "Notes sur *Madame Bovary*." *L'Arc* 79 (1979): 38–43.

Schehr, Lawrence R. *Flaubert and Sons.* New York: Peter Lang, 1987.

Schor, Naomi. *Breaking the Chains: Women, Theory, and French Realist Fiction.* New York: Columbia University Press, 1985.

———. "Details and Decadence: End-Troping in *Madame Bovary*." *Sub-stance* 26 (1980): 27–35.

Schor, Naomi, and Henry F. Majewski, eds. *Flaubert and Post-modernism.* Lincoln: University of Nebraska Press, 1984.

Sherrington, R. J. *Three Novels by Flaubert: A Study of Techniques.* Oxford: Clarendon, 1970.

Steegmuller, Francis. *Flaubert and Madame Bovary: A Double Portrait.* New York: Viking, 1939.

Tanner, Tony. *Adultery in the Novel: Contract and Transgression.* Baltimore: Johns Hopkins University Press, 1979.

Terdiman, Richard. "Flaubert and After: Failure Formalized." In *The Dialectics of Isolation: Self and Society in the French Novel from the Realists to Proust,* 60–90. New Haven: Yale University Press, 1976.

Thibaudet, Albert. *Gustave Flaubert.* Paris: Gallimard, 1935.

Thornton, Lawrence. "The Fairest of Them All: Modes of Vision in *Madame Bovary*." *PMLA* 93 (1978): 982–91.

Weinberg, Henry H. "The Function of Italics in *Madame Bovary*." *Nineteenth-Century French Studies* 3 (1974): 97–111.

Wetherill, P. M. "*Madame Bovary*'s Blind Man: Symbolism in Flaubert." *Romanic Review* 61 (1970): 35–42.

Williams, D. A. *Psychological Determinism in* Madame Bovary. Yorkshire: University of Hull, 1973.

———. "The Role of Binet in *Madame Bovary*." *Romanic Review* 71 (1980): 149–66.

Acknowledgments

"The Tragedy of Dreams" (originally entitled "*Madame Bovary:* The Tragedy of Dreams") by Victor Brombert from *The Novels of Flaubert: A Study of Themes and Techniques* by Victor Brombert, © 1966 by Princeton University Press. Reprinted by permission of Princeton University Press.

"Flaubert and Emma Bovary: The Hazards of Literary Fusion" by Leo Bersani from *Towards a Poetics of Fiction,* edited by Mark Spilka, © 1977 by Indiana University Press. Reprinted by permission of Indiana University Press.

"The 'Morselization' of Emma Bovary" (originally entitled "Flaubert's *Madame Bovary*") by Tony Tanner from *Adultery in the Novel: Contract and Transgression* by Tony Tanner. © 1979 by The Johns Hopkins University Press, Baltimore/London. Reprinted by permission of The Johns Hopkins University Press.

"For a Restricted Thematics: Writing, Speech and Difference in *Madame Bovary*" by Naomi Schor from *The Future of Difference,* edited by Hester Eisenstein and Alice Jardine, © 1980 by Naomi Schor. Reprinted by permission. This essay was translated by Harriet Stone.

"The Biographer as Literary Critic: Sartre's Flaubert and *Madame Bovary*" (originally entitled "*Madame Bovary*") by Hazel Barnes from *Sartre and Flaubert* by Hazel Barnes, © 1981 by the University of Chicago. Reprinted by permission of the University of Chicago Press.

"The Trial" by Dominick LaCapra from Madame Bovary *on Trial* by Dominick LaCapra, © 1982 by Cornell University Press. Reprinted by permission of the publisher, Cornell University Press.

"Narrative Strategies in *Madame Bovary*" (originally entitled "*Madame Bovary*") by Michal Peled Ginsburg from *Flaubert Writing: A Study in Narrative Strategies* by Michal Peled Ginsburg, © 1986 by the Board of Trustees of the Leland Stanford Junior University. Reprinted by permission of the publisher, Stanford University Press.

Index